STUDIES IN FAULKNER

STUDIES IN

FAULKNER

Ann L. Hayes   John A. Hart   Ralph A. Ciancio
Beekman W. Cottrell   Neal Woodruff, Jr.

6

CARNEGIE SERIES IN ENGLISH

Essay Index Reprint Series

BOOKS FOR LIBRARIES PRESS
FREEPORT, NEW YORK

Library of Congress Cataloging in Publication Data

Carnegie Institute of Technology, Pittsburgh. Dept. of
    English.
    Studies in Faulkner.

    (Essay index reprint series)
    Original ed. issued as no. 6 of the Carnegie series
in English.
    Includes bibliographical references.
    1. Faulkner, William, 1897-1962. I. Hayes, Ann L.
II. Title. III. Series: Carnegie series in English,
no. 6.
[PS3511.A86Z754 1972]   813'.5'2   72-1325
ISBN 0-8369-2839-3

PS
3511
A86
Z754
1972

Foreword

Number Six in the Carnegie Series in English consists of five critical studies of the works of William Faulkner by members of the Department of English. No attempt has been made to achieve consistency of approach or to eliminate disagreement, and the writers of the papers are sometimes at variance.

The authors are grateful to Random House, Inc., for permission to quote from their editions of the works of Faulkner listed at the end of the volume, and to Simon and Schuster, Inc., for permission to quote a passage from *The Greek Passion*, by Nikos Kazanzakis, copyright 1954 by Simon and Schuster, Inc.

The papers were prepared for the press by an editorial committee consisting of Neal Woodruff, Jr. (Chairman), Norman Knox, and A. Fred Sochatoff.

Publication of this volume has been made possible by a grant from the Wherrett Memorial Fund of the Pittsburgh Foundation. For this vital assistance the Department of English is deeply grateful.

AUSTIN WRIGHT, *Head*
Department of English

Contents

STUDIES IN FAULKNER

THE WORLD OF THE HAMLET

ANN L. HAYES

THE CRITICAL HISTORY OF *The Hamlet* is mixed. It has been commended as Faulkner's truly comic book, a blend of tall tale and farce in the ancient tradition of folk comedy.[1] It has also been described as the unattractive doings of as unattractive a village as one would care to meet.[2] The most famous account is Malcolm Cowley's description of it as a series of episodes strung together like beads on a string.[3] This is a remark epitomizing one judgment of *The Hamlet*, a judgment which can be supported by reference to the novel. Certainly it contains a variety of episodes, and its parts are separable enough that several of them first appeared as independent short stories.[4] They are also separable enough that the long third section could

---

[1] William Van O'Connor, *The Tangled Fire of William Faulkner* (Minneapolis, 1954), pp. 162-163.

[2] Stephen Vincent Benet, review of *The Hamlet, Saturday Review of Literature*, XXI (April 6, 1940), 7.

[3] Malcolm Cowley, "Introduction," *The Portable Faulkner* (New York, 1946), p. 18.

[4] The novel uses the following short stories in revised form: "Fool About a Horse," *Scribner's*, 1936—pp. 33-53, *The Hamlet*; "The Hound," *Dr. Martino*, 1934—pp. 250-296; "Spotted Horses," *Scribner's*, 1931—pp. 309-380; "Lizards in Jamshyd's Courtyard," *Saturday Evening Post*, 1932—pp. 383-421. In addition parts of other stories have been used: "Barn Burning," *Harper's*, 1939— pp. 15-21; a paragraph from *The Unvanquished*—p. 33; "Afternoon of a Cow" in manuscript in June, 1937, but not published until after publication of the novel—pp. 197-199. See also William Van O'Connor's summary of the literary history in *Tangled Fire*, p. 176, and information given by James B. Meriwether, "William Faulkner: A Check List," *Princeton University Library Chronicle*, XVIII (1957), 137-150.

be sold as the basis for a film. Furthermore, the book is best known not as a whole but for some of its parts: for the brilliance of the spotted horses story, or the unorthodox lyric of Ike Snopes's romance.

Yet of the three books in which the fortunes of the Snopes family are traced, *The Hamlet* is the most satisfactory as a novel. The progress of Flem Snopes begins in Frenchman's Bend, in *The Hamlet*, and continues in Jefferson, in *The Town* and *The Mansion*. What his progress means is the theme of all three novels, but it is given its most effective and direct statement in the first. The events in *The Town* and *The Mansion* tell what else happens, what men do with their lives, and how at last Flem fails in his adherence to what he represents, and is destroyed. Our belief in what happens, however, is rooted in the first novel. It is *The Hamlet* which creates a world and makes it real.

The basis of such a second judgment of the novel has also been given focus by a critical remark, also famous. In an essay which grew out of his long review of *The Portable Faulkner* Robert Penn Warren suggests of *The Hamlet* that "in the novel we have a type of organization in which the thematic rather than the narrative emphasis is the basic principle. . ." and again, of Faulkner's other pieces as well as this, that "we may sometimes discover the true unity if we think of the line of meaning, the symbolic ordering, and surrender ourselves to the tale-teller's 'voice.' "[5] Those who have found meaningful unity in *The Hamlet* have since worked out Warren's suggestion in considerable detail.[6] In defense of their position, they can point out that any novel is a series of events. When the unifying emphasis in the novel is upon the relationship of the events, the series strikes us as episodes in one story. When the emphasis is upon their meaning, the series will seem to fall apart if we are looking for the narrative emphasis which is not there. The sense of unity returns when we notice the alternative, thematic means of organization.

[5] Robert Penn Warren, "William Faulkner," *William Faulkner: Three Decades of Criticism*, ed. Frederick J. Hoffman and Olga W. Vickery (East Lansing, Mich., 1960), p. 123.
[6] Such discussions include essays by Russell Roth, "The Centaur and the Pear Tree," *Western Review*, XVI (1952), 199-205; Peter Lisca, "*The Hamlet*: Genesis and Revisions," *Faulkner Studies*, III (1954), 5-13; Viola Hopkins, "Meaning and Form in Faulkner's *The Hamlet*," *Accent*, XV (1955), 125-144; Florence Leaver, "The Structure of *The Hamlet*," *Twentieth Century Literature*, I (1955), 77-84; T. Y. Greet, "The Theme and Structure of Faulkner's *The Hamlet*," *PMLA*, LXII (1957), 775-790, and since reprinted in *Three Decades of Criticism*; Floyd C. Watkins and Thomas Daniel Young, "Revisions of Style in Faulkner's *The Hamlet*," *Modern Fiction Studies*, V (1959-60), 327-336; Olga W. Vickery, "The Profit and the Loss: *The Hamlet* and *The Town*" in *The Novels of William Faulkner* (Baton Rouge, La., 1959).

Faulkner certainly does not present a single orderly time-scheme in *The Hamlet*. Of the three novels it has the least chronological order. Neither does it have an unchanging focus on any person. What it does focus on is the assault on Frenchman's Bend by the Snopes world, especially by its chief representative, Flem Snopes. By this means, Faulkner considers the quality which he names "rapacity." It occurs in most Snopeses, but in varying degrees. In Flem it is pure, undefiled by any commitment to anything else. In his relatives it is modified in various ways. That the study of rapacity is the theme of *The Hamlet*, and that the novel gains its unity from its thematic structure, is evident when its parts are considered with this possibility in mind, for then, instead of being "beads on a string," they are the related phrases of a whole statement. Each book of the four-part novel illumines what the hamlet is, suggests what it might be, and shows what Snopesism does to it: by this means each book illumines the nature and effect of rapacity.

In the first book, the hamlet and the Snopes family are introduced, and so are the power and morality each represents. The symbol of economic power in the hamlet is Will Varner, who is its principal landowner and businessman. He represents its morality, too, but not its most enlightened morality. The symbol of that is V. K. Ratliff, who does not live in the hamlet but is accepted there as a member of the community and makes part of his living there. Flem Snopes is the symbol of both the power and the morality of his family: the power is like Varner's, economic and shrewd; the morality is opportunism, a perfect willingness to use whatever comes along. The first book is the narrative of the initial skirmishes between Frenchman's Bend and the Snopes family; when we reach its conclusion, we know something of the nature and meaning of each.

If we look primarily for a narrative connection, the relation between the first book and the second is puzzling, for a new central figure is introduced and Flem Snopes drops nearly out of sight for some time. Eula Varner's story is not told as a continuation of the story in Book I, but as an addition to it. It begins earlier than the events in the first book, and continues past them, although the two narratives do merge when the second book picks up the story of the first at a later time and continues it. The events of the book do continue the story of the hamlet, however, for they tell us, through symbol, what the hamlet might have won: the richness and promise that might have been fulfilled, but that turned into just one more way to get ahead, unvalued in itself. Faulkner shifts from an economic to a sexual image, but he does not entirely dissociate the two; he uses both when Flem

Snopes marries Eula Varner, taking her away from the hamlet, although he never possesses her. Faulkner makes clear, however, that this is not only a triumph of Flem's astuteness. The hamlet loses Eula to Snopesism, but it had proved unequal to her in any case: it lost her first to an outsider, who disappeared, before losing her finally to the interloper who is present at the right moment and convenient to take her away.

As narrative, the third book also seems disjunctive, for it is not about Flem or Eula; they are not even present. Instead, it is about other members of the Snopes family and other citizens of the hamlet. Their loves and hatreds contrast with the flat absence of feeling which the earlier books have established for Flem. Snopeses attack the hamlet in their various ways, scrabbling at keeping alive and getting ahead; yet the rapacity shown unrelieved in Flem is modified in them, not only by their various incapacities, but also by their capacity for feeling. Book III thus develops the infection of the village, which continues now whether Flem is there or not. For one thing, Flem has made a place in the community and although he is away, he is talked about; further, he has changed the world he entered by introducing other members of the Snopes family into it. Lump Snopes runs the store, I.O. is the school teacher, Eck is in the blacksmith shop, Mink farms what he correctly guesses to be Flem's land. None of this is digression. Faulkner develops what being a Snopes is, analyzing various Snopes lives and opposing them to non-Snopes lives and to the commentary of Ratliff. There is no need to confine what he calls rapacity to one man. Yet these other men are not purely rapacious; the capacity for feeling, in them and in others, makes up the narrative of this book. It is full of the life that sheer getting and owning can never know.

Thematically, the novel is still coherent; seen this way, the fourth book brings to it both narrative and thematic unity. We know now that Faulkner is not concerned with the everyday meanness and sharp dealing of the Varners, which a man can gauge and expect, but with imperviousness to the rights and needs of others. Flem demonstrates such imperviousness. He and Eula return; the symbolism of Eula as lost promise is repeated; and the triumph of Flem is complete when he gulls the hamlet by the sale of the spotted horses and then gulls Ratliff by the device of the salted goldmine. Flem gets ahead. He leaves behind him a village infested by Snopeses, tricked of its money, partly maimed. At the end of the novel, Flem moves off toward Jefferson, with Eula in the buggy beside him. We have watched Faulkner isolate a negative quality: a complete absence of morality which is an absence of being. Flem exists only as he is rapacious. *The Hamlet* creates this quality, not as a definition of an abstraction or as an allegory, but by a fictional demonstration of what it is and means, the story of some people and what they did. Faulkner's complex telling and retelling creates the world from which abstractions take life. It is not only by consistent development of theme that the novel creates unity. Its singleness of effect depends just as much on the consistent feeling of dismay and dislike Faulkner expresses toward Snopesism. He conveys this best by creating a contrasting character, V. K. Ratliff, and by making him an occasional narrator, a critical commenter on the Snopes family. Ratliff is a man of perceptive intelligence, informed with sympathy and understanding. Like Flem, he makes his living by knowing what other people want. He travels through the county, selling sewing machines and trading, carrying news and messages, learning the secrets and desires of his customers as he goes. It is his business to know what is wanted and what is going on, yet he is not an exploiter. He supplies a need in the county and gives fair value for what he takes; this is supported by the trust and respect which he commands and by the relation he bears to other characters. He could travel around the county for a month without buying a meal, we are told, and Will Varner discusses his own motives and concerns with him as he is not shown doing with any other person. Ratliff does not live in Frenchman's Bend, but he is a member of the community as Flem is not. He not only understands its customs and standards, he operates within them. A man dealing with him takes his chances, but he knows what they are, and he knows that if he keeps his wits about him he can make a fair trade. Thinking about a friend's attempt to warn him once, Ratliff shows his moral sensitivity and his awareness of the limits on action which it imposes: "He done all he could to warn me. He went as far and even further than a man can let his self go in another man's trade" (94).[7] Ratliff also on occasion transcends the community. He is not a customer in the day's trading for spotted horses, although most of his customers are; when the sodomy of Ike Snopes becomes public, he is the one who makes what arrangements he can for Ike's welfare.

The creation of Ratliff and the role he is given as opposition to Flem Snopes are, then, commentaries on Snopesism. Ratliff is always shrewd, amiable, accepted by the community; although he acts independently, his opposition to Flem is accepted by the community. In its very simplest terms, the judgment Faulkner makes between the characters is always the same: Ratliff—yes; Flem—no. But the commentary is one informed with humor;

---

[7] All page references given in the text are to *The Hamlet*.

Faulkner's consistent dislike and dismay do not preclude his laughter: in fact the tradition is that Faulkner and his friend Phil Stone "worked up the Snopes saga in a spirit of anecdotal whimsy. Models," as Stone puts it, "were at hand in and around Oxford."[8] *The Hamlet* is dedicated to Stone.

To this consistency of attitude toward the characters is added Ratliff's narrative voice, "a pleasant, lazy, equable voice which you did not discern at once to be even more shrewd than humorous" (14). He begins talking early in the first book. He is the principal source of information about the Snopes family and where they have been before their sudden appearance in Frenchman's Bend. He summarizes for Jody Varner the arrival of Ab Snopes and his family as share-croppers on a farm elsewhere in the county, and the subsequent quarrel and barn-burning. (The story he tells is also told in the short story "Barn-Burning.") Later he sums up the situation for Will Varner. " 'I think the same as you do. . . . That there aint but two men I know can risk fooling with them folks. And just one of them is named Varner and his front name aint Jody.' 'And who's the other one?' Varner said. 'That aint been proved yet neither,' Ratliff said pleasantly" (31). He means by the first, Will Varner, and by the second, himself. Between them they represent the strength of the hamlet: each can risk combat with Flem Snopes; but neither has yet proved he can win. Again, Ratliff gives information to the men lounging at the store. To them he tells an earlier story of Ab Snopes, sketching his bushwhacker background (this is part of the Ab Snopes story told in *The Unvanquished*) and then going on to the horse-trading epic of Snopes and Pat Stamper, when, as Ratliff tells it, "Pat eliminated him from horse-trading. And so he just went plumb curdled" (33). (This is also told in "Fool About a Horse.") Ratliff's diction is dialectal, his sentences show consistent rearrangements of grammatical patterns, but it is the tone he establishes that matters most: easy, unemphatic, the voice of an observer who waits behind the flow of words to see whether his listeners understand. It is a tone used over and over in *The Hamlet*, given to Ratliff to establish but constantly recurring in Faulkner's own voice as well as in his characters' voices.

The recurring, consistent contrast between Ratliff and Flem is a unifying force in more than its statement of attitude. It serves as an image of the conflict between the world of an imperfect civilization and the world of no civilization at all, which each represents. For instance, the business methods of the two are deliberately contrasted. Ratliff's, demonstrated on his trip

---

[8] Harry Modean Campbell and Ruel E. Foster, *William Faulkner: A Critical Appraisal* (Norman, Okla., 1951), p. 102.

around the county and into the next state, are based on his shrewd knowledge of others, but it is a knowledge which admits credit, kinship, reasonable trust in barter and trade; and his success needs an amicable, reciprocal relationship with others. Sometimes all he retails is news, but this is as important as anything he does, and he exchanges information just as he trades notes and goods. Flem, on the other hand, running Varner's store for "customers who had traded there for years, mostly serving themselves and putting the correct change into the cigar box inside the cheese cage" (64), is conducting a business which admits no trust whatsoever. He sees to each transaction, makes no mistakes, and answers yes or no to direct questions. He has even refused credit to a man "who had been into and out of the store's debt at least once a year for the last fifteen" (65)—and this time brought Will Varner galloping in to assert that the store is still his own, or that, as one of the farmers puts it, he thinks it is.

The contrast is repeated in another way. Issue is joined between the two men in the form of a trade with Flem by which Ratliff will redeem two notes given him by Mink Snopes. It is on their opposite responses to Ike Snopes, the idiot, that the deal turns. The two characters of Flem and Ratliff are again etched. Flem uses the idiot just as he uses everyone else, as something convenient and negotiable. Ratliff treats him as the subject of special compassion. Ratliff therefore makes no profit by the deal, but it is his own choice, and he confirms to Will Varner his earlier remark: "Just tell him Ratliff says it aint been proved yet neither" (101). Matters between the ethical intelligence which Ratliff represents and the perfect opportunism which is Flem are for the present in balance.

The contrast is continued, and the balance is resolved, in the two stories of the last book, which tells Flem's triumph over Frenchman's Bend. In the first chapter, the revision of the famous "Spotted Horses," the community betrays itself out of its own desires and needs. Flem is apart, doing very little. The Texan conducts the sale and no one knows for certain that the ponies belong to Flem, although everyone, including Ratliff, assumes that they do. Ratliff watches and comments the night before the sale. "All right. You folks can buy them critters if you want to. But me, I'd just as soon buy a tiger or a rattlesnake. And if Flem Snopes offered me either one of them, I would be afraid to touch it for fear it would turn out to be a painted dog or a piece of garden hose when I went up to take possession of it" (318). As he put it earlier, in another trade, he done all he could to warn them. He is not present for the sale itelf, but returns that evening and is part of the comic and violent turmoil of the attempt to catch the horses. He is

10 STUDIES IN FAULKNER

the one who goes for Will Varner to set Henry Armstid's broken leg, and the one who talks Lump Snopes into letting slip that the horses were in fact Flem's. In the matter of Mrs. Armstid's five dollars, it is Ratliff who tells her story so that Flem can hear it.

It has been said that Ratliff's defeat by Flem in the final section of the novel makes the character a "marred triumph" since it is not credible that Ratliff, who knows Flem so well and has so vigorously expressed his contempt and understanding, should at last be fooled by him and betrayed by his own avarice.[9] It is true that Ratliff "had never for one moment believed that [the Old Frenchman place] had no value" (179). He repeats this conviction to Bookwright at the beginning of their adventure together. "There's something there. I've always knowed it. Just like Will Varner knows there is something there. If there wasn't, he wouldn't never have bought it. And he wouldn't a kept it . . ." (384). This is some preparation for Ratliff's delusion, but not enough. It provides the bait that Flem is using, for Ratliff like every other victim deludes himself; Flem provides the opportunity, and profits from it. The explanation for Ratliff's defeat does not lie in his character, as it should, but in the theme Faulkner is developing. Thematically, it is Ratliff's success, not his failure, to be fooled by Flem. Flem's shrewdness is his weapon: what he engages in is undeterred action resulting from unimpaired perception. He is a man always alert to take what he wants as soon as he sees it. Because he has no sense of his own dignity as a human being, only of his status as agent, he takes any step which heads away from the sharecropper's field. He does not have to plan ahead except to store away possible sources of advantage as they occur. When the time comes to use an advantage, a time dictated by circumstance, then he uses it simply and directly, concerned only with efficacy. The concept is familiar in Faulkner. Seeing, stripped of every modifying feeling, is irresistibly successful; and Flem's eyes are "stagnant water" with which there is no communication, flat disks which tell the world nothing, for he is sane and only sane. He is untouched by any loyalty or any tradition; having power that other Snopeses do not have because he has intelligence they do not have, he exploits even his family. Against him stands the figure of Ratliff, observant, shrewd, informed with a sense of the value of a man. He is distinguished from the community which Flem preys upon because he is not victimized; instead he sees, warns, sometimes takes counter action, and has once at least come out even with Flem in a trade. When he too is

[9] Irving Howe, *William Faulkner: A Critical Study* (New York, 1952), p. 183.

gulled by Flem, he returns fully to the community; Flem alone is the other. And Ratliff's knowledge, though expensive, is complete. The logic of the situation does not make it easier to accept Ratliff's being fooled. The development of both narrative and theme demands that Flem should triumph; only the character of Ratliff leaves us uncertain and dissatisfied that things could have turned out this way.

The contrast between the two men supplies one unifying image; the Old Frenchman place itself supplies another. We begin with it and end with it; its ownership changes twice, each time for a critical reason. It is a symbol of past greatness, now unregarded and anonymous, important to the countryside at the beginning of the novel for the story of gold that haunts it and for the mild curiosity created by Will Varner's owning it. This ownership coalesces images of past and present power, for Varner, at the opening of the novel, is the chief man of the community and sits, apparently idle, on the lawn or porch of the Old Frenchman place knowing the business of two counties. Ratliff too enters here; it is Ratliff to whom Varner gives his reasons for sitting on there—one of them that he is trying "to find out what it must have felt like to be the fool that would need all this . . . just to eat and sleep in" (7). Together, the ruined mansion, Varner, and Ratliff are the symbols of the world into which Flem Snopes moves. The mansion is part of the past, almost wholly without value now except as men create new dreams around it. Varner is the self-willed authority of the present society, not particularly good, running its business and dispensing its justice, "a farmer, a usurer, a veterinarian" and "the largest landholder and beat supervisor in one county and Justice of the Peace in the next and election commissioner in both, and hence the fountainhead if not of law at least of advice and suggestion . . ." (5). Beyond this, he "owned most of the good land in the country and held mortgages on most of the rest. He owned the store and the cotton gin and the combined grist mill and blacksmith shop in the village proper and it was considered, to put it mildly, bad luck for a man of the neighborhood to do his trading or gin his cotton or grind his meal or shoe his stock anywhere else" (5-6). Compared with Varner, Ratliff has a private position and function: he knows the countryside, what it wants and what it is willing to pay; he is a man who learns secrets because it is his passion and business to know. The two men between them embody the ethical responsibility of the Frenchman's Bend world: both are shrewd, tough, unsentimental, concerned with their own affairs, but operating within a system known to themselves and their world. When Flem Snopes takes over the Old Frenchman place as Eula's dowry, and when he in turn sells

it to Armstid and Bookwright and Ratliff by means of the old trick of the
salted goldmine, a symbol of the past is changing hands. Faulkner does
not underline this or comment on it, but his handling of the imagery is
characteristic: this house had been the center of a great pre-Civil War plantation, where there had been not only lands but stables, slave quarters,
gardens, terraces, promenades. The river bed had been straightened for almost ten miles by slaves to keep the land from flooding; its course and the
ruined, ransacked house are all that remain. This remnant of great achieve-
ment and magnificent scope now is part of the price of a marriage and then
exploited as a greedy hope to get something for nothing.

For the same reason that Faulkner's conception of Flem is one which
invites the use of contrast, the conception creates a less dominant image
than might be expected. Flem is a figure of evil in traditional terms, cut
off from what is decent and human not by what he is but by what he is not.
He has intelligence without responsibility, desire without love; he does not
even know what he wants, only what he does not want. He is menacing
not because he has a positive power but because he does not have any of
the usual human responses; what is evil about him is a negation of being,
a failure to be. It is remarkable, for instance, how little he ever does. His
skill is to see the opportunity and then to be in the right place; after that
he lets his victims defeat themselves. Flem's rise begins with someone else's
fear. He succeeds in taking away all that Jody Varner has because Jody is
not intelligent enough or brave enough to cut his first losses; Jody's fear
that he will lose his barn and his hay is what makes his loss possible. The
rise continues because Flem sees and takes each successive step of advantage,
yet gives no one any possible hold or claim upon him. He can be attacked
only through his own weakness, and he shows none. He moves into the
store and then moves into the village and then brings his relatives without
ever giving or asking anything. He does not even look at other people or
eat with other people; he has no part in the civilized relationships of a community, even Frenchman's Bend. When he affects the signs of dignity he
is both ludicrous and menacing, for his white shirt and store-made bowtie
can be only symbols of power. Faulkner confirms this effect by his use of
detail: the new white shirt is streaked with the creases of the bolt of cloth
from which it was cut. So is the next shirt which replaces it at the end of
the week and which soils in exactly the same way the first had. "It was as
though its wearer, entering though he had into a new life and milieu already
channeled to compulsions and customs fixed long before his advent, had
nevertheless established in it even on that first day his own particular soiling

groove" (58). The bowtie too has its peculiar menace. It is just "a tiny machine-made black bow which snapped together at the back with a metal fastener" (66). Will Varner owns the only other tie in the whole Frenchman's Bend country; Flem is to wear this or one like it, we are told, until his death—"a tiny viciously depthless cryptically balanced splash like an enigmatic punctuation symbol . . ." (66).

The contrast with Ratliff states Faulkner's judgment of Flem and of Snopesism, but does not solve a narrative problem. Ratliff is not a primary source of action and neither is Flem. Following the narrative of Flem's arrival and establishment and the preliminary encounter between him and Ratliff, what is needed is a series of stories about other persons which will develop the theme further. This is precisely what we get. When we begin the story all over again with Eula we turn from an encounter in moral terms to what is mostly a description of a nonmoral force. She is like some fertility goddess, or, as Labove says, "the fine land rich and fecund and foul and eternal and impervious to him who claimed title to it . . ." (135). Labove's story is told because his is a fierce but human ambition. He can make gifts to his family, recognize and honor contracts, try to act within a community's expectations, which might be called at least the remnants of a moral code, and he can recognize Eula, need her, and be defeated by her oblivion and inertia. By what Labove is and understands, by what Eula is, Faulkner implies what Flem is not. Then the young men of the countryside become aware of Eula, court her, and lose her to McCarron, the outsider. Their loss and the loss of all the community is Flem Snopes's gain, one more advantage accepted, although its ultimate value cannot be reckoned. What Flem can accomplish out of others' weakness and needs is detailed in Book I; what he might have and does not have is told in Book II, the story of what Eula herself does not know she is and of what everyone loses. Flem's peculiar loss is that he does not admit there was anything important to lose; he has no part in the loss, although it is fertility itself, the land with its promise, that is wasted when Flem takes possession of it.

The stories of other persons may be the stories of others in the family, for Flem is not the only Snopes. He is rapacity unmodified by any other quality; but Faulkner shows us the Snopes family in a spectrum from Flem at one end to Ike at the other. The idyll of Ike and the cow, almost totally non-human as it is, is filled with sympathy for need and blindness and loneliness. Ike's responses are entirely feeling, instinctive, modified by no judgment. Even hope and despair are for him nearly unperceivable; he cannot understand what he wants or why he reacts, and without reason he simply gives himself to love. Faulkner writes his summer day as a long, lyrical description. The situation is farce, but instead of concentrating on the comic, Faulkner fixes on the loveliness of the Mississippi countryside into which he lets his odd lovers sink. Ike's elysium is given in terms of nature and of natural things—sunshine, rain, dappled shade, the sweet grain—as if in his love he makes himself wholly a part of the natural world. The romantic treatment is consistent and true to Faulkner's view of the world; it is not Ike's longing which is seen as perversion, but the reaction of the community to it. Lump Snopes, who can understand the whole situation, realizes that he may make a little out of it by prying loose a board in the backfence. "He pulled that plank off! At just exactly the right height! Not child-height and not woman-height: man-height!" Ratliff cries (226). When Ike and the cow are back in Frenchman's Bend they are a sideshow, but it is those who have neither sympathy nor scruples who have made them one. In those terms the relationship comes back into the normal framework; under such conditions it is Ike who remains sympathetic and pitiable.

Significantly, Ike is the only Snopes treated with tenderness, and he reveals the quality of each person who deals with him. Flem trades a note for Ike's ten-dollar inheritance, as does Mink, before Ratliff destroys it. Later, Houston and Ratliff both are defined as men by their response to the idiot in his need. Houston, outraged and furious, gets Ike out of the creek and washes his overalls for him. Ratliff nails the boards back in the fence and then does what he can for Ike's welfare. The schoolteacher, I. O. Snopes, condones Lump's peepshow arrangements until Ratliff points out that this may cost him his job; I. O. arranges then that someone else bear the cost of buying the cow and ending the affair. On the argument of the value of the Snopes name, Eck is persuaded to pay the bill. By this Eck demonstrates that he is no Snopes. Not only is he easily defrauded by his uncle (or cousin) I. O., but he feels enough compassion for Ike to buy him the wooden toy with which Ike is last seen.[1]

There are other stories of the family. I. O., who is a true Snopes, defiles the community both by his fathering of "big, gray-colored chaps" (Clarence, Vardaman, Bilbo and Montgomery Ward Snopes are among these) and by his corruption of language. A stream of platitude and misquotation is his natural talk. I. O. and Lump are less successful copies of what Flem is—a forgery, Ratliff calls Lump—introduced mainly as examples of what Flem

---

[1] That Eck is not a Snopes, indicated here in *The Hamlet*, is spelled out in *The Town*. Neither he nor his son Wallstreet Panic belongs to the tribe. Wall, indeed, as his story in the later novel explains, is in opposition to it; and Eck is crippled behaving gallantly in a stupid accident—a situation in which no Snopes would be found.

has drawn into the community after him. The Snopes family appears and spreads, filling each job as Flem moves on to a new one, so that by the time Flem leaves Frenchman's Bend for the conquest of Jefferson they are ready to follow him from the hamlet to the town.[2]

Ike, Abner, and Mink (unlike I. O. and Lump) are all useful to Faulkner for what they are that Flem is not, and their stories are all told in detail. Ike's particular quality we have seen; Ab's "fierce intractability" and anger against injustice have made a barn-burner of him, but compared with Flem's impassivity, these true qualities are almost admirable. As Ratliff tells the story of Ab's deal with the great trader Pat Stamper, Ab is a marked and doomed man: "It was fate. It was like the Lord Himself had decided to buy a horse with Miz Snopes's separator money. Though I will admit that when He chose Ab He picked out a good quick willing hand to do His trading for Him" (36). Ab's bitter pride is a preparation for the ferocity of Mink Snopes, who feels that in murdering Jack Houston he is asserting "his rights as a man and his feelings as a sentient creature" (251), who would have liked to print a placard *"This is what happens to the men who impound Mink Snopes's cattle"* (250-251), sign his name to it and leave it on Houston's breast. Even the wildly macabre duel between Mink and the hound fits into Faulkner's saga of Snopes, for it illustrates, as Ab's fury does for him, a way in which Mink at least *is*: to be Ab, or Mink, or Ike is better, Faulkner is saying, than to be Flem. It is better to endure a perversion of a human feeling—pride or hatred or love—than to be impotent of any feeling at all. It is worth adding to this certain tentative generalizations about Faulkner's evaluation of intelligence. Ike, who has no reason, still has instinctive responses which those who can make abstractions can call devotion and courage and fidelity. Instinct without intelligence, in Ike, is pitiable; intelligence controlling and serving emotion and instinct, in Houston and Ratliff, is admirable; intelligence without feeling, in Flem, or so far as it exists, in Lump or I. O., is contemptible.

In the light of the narrative problem, it is not surprising that there are so many love stories in *The Hamlet*. The story of Mink himself is partly a love story, if a picaresque one. Mink shows mostly a possessive desire, but this is more real to him as a sense of himself than his need to escape being

---

2 At the end of the first skirmish in Jefferson, told in *The Town*, Flem is quietly doing what Ratliff describes as "farming Snopeses," making his living from relatives drawn after him into town. This is temporary. No Snopes is safe from a Snopes or useful to a Snopes solely because of the family relationship. When Flem finds that he must rephrase the quality which has brought him money if it is also to give him respectability, he demonstrates his knowledge by clearing first Montgomery Ward Snopes and then I. O. out of Jefferson.

tried for murder, and he throws away the money his wife has earned which might provide escape. His wife, although she can be free of him, chooses to stay in Jefferson and wait through his winter in jail and his trial. Jack Houston's too is a love story. He runs away from Lucy Pate but "He fled, not from his past, but to escape his future. It took him twelve years to learn you cannot escape either of them" (242). Then, having returned to her and married her, he loses her; but at the time of his death over four years later he is still regulating his life to control his grief for her. Lying "rigid, indomitable, and panting" on his cot, he can say, " I dont understand it. I dont know why. I wont ever know why. But You cant beat me. I am as strong as You are. You cant beat me" (248-249). Both of these stories contrast with the entirely selfless love of Ike Snopes, related in the same book. The various lovers are in contrast too with Eula Varner and the men who have loved her. All of those who are able to enter such a relationship with each other are in contrast with Flem.

Despite the variety of episode and the changing narrative techniques, Faulkner examines a single subject and maintains a consistent attitude toward it. *The Hamlet* tells the story of an invasion of evil into a world which is not very good. It is not a series of stories, but a novel, if we are willing to substitute for the development of a single action the development of a single idea—what Faulkner means by rapacity. Once we accept that, the novel has the clear unity of thematic organization and consistent judgment. What Faulkner says occurred to him in separate parts, it is true, but the parts are phrases in one statement, a coherent image of a world.

FAULKNER'S COSMIC FABLE

THE EXTRAORDINARY FAMILY OF MAN

BEEKMAN W. COTTRELL

AT LEAST ONCE before he dies, each great writer seems impelled to set down, or to try to set down, his broadest vision of the world and its meaning. Where he has heretofore been content to create life and people in accordance with his own view of reality, he now wishes to add, consciously, another element, the element of judgment. This is not always accomplished through editorializing, though that function often takes on greater importance in such poems or plays or novels. The sense of cosmic purpose, the overall moral vision of the writer, pervades more strongly than ever before the characters and events of the story. The bounds of the artist widen in such cosmic works; he tries more, ranges more widely, dares infinitely. He seems driven by a sense of urgency to show and tell all, grasping at the sleeve of the reader like a veritable ancient mariner, using every device at his command to try to ennoble and heighten and widen and deepen the work at hand, and to convince the reader that its meaning is of great importance.

Because it oversteps traditional boundaries, the cosmic novel rarely "succeeds." Or to put it another way, such a novel tries to achieve so much that it is almost bound to "fail." Flaubert's *The Temptation of Saint Anthony*, Melville's *Pierre*, George Eliot's *Daniel Deronda*, the late novels of Henry James, to some degree *The Brothers Karamazov*, *The Magic Mountain*, *Docter Faustus*, *Nostromo* and *Ulysses*—these books and others like them stand apart, perhaps above, in any case detached from the real world of most fiction. They offer a vision and an answer—or they put immense questions which can lead the reader to achieve an answer. Their scope is large, and most of them are long. More important, these novels are very wide in implication. Many are, almost perforce, unwieldly in structure or "imperfect" in form. One can often perceive that the author has seen an inner or an overall structure more clearly than his readers at first may see. And sometimes the reader senses that the writer no longer cares: he who was hitherto concerned with balance and proportion now has felt his subject—the Meaning of Life—to be more important than form or manner, and has been ready to risk lack of understanding, repetition, self-parody, even ridicule, to have his say.

At the same time, such cosmic attempts always offer unique rewards. They reread profitably because so much of the author's intensity and complexity has gone into them. At their best, they offer new insights with study. They are often exciting philosophically, and they are always memorable. What primarily unites these cosmic statements about the world is the immense and intense concern of their writers. It is a concern which overrides tradition in the novel, and attempts to prove that experiment and scope and outright philosophical speculation can have a valid place in fiction. The felt concern is meant to overbalance any lack of the more generally accepted limits of prose fiction—some kind of traditional structure or unity, believable characters, and lifelike events. Perhaps all must be judged flawed masterpieces, unless the critic denies that disproportion or imperfection can exist in a masterpiece. But from the author's point of view, the word *masterpiece*—carefully divided—is exact.

Such a flawed masterpiece is *A Fable*. Monumental, intense, finely balanced and in part deeply moving, it is composed of all the elements which go to make up Faulkner's genius. Its basic story is centered on the false armistice in May of 1918, and the novel supplies an ingenious explanation for that phenomenon. Led by a corporal of Middle European origin—now in the French army—and his squad, an entire regiment (and in turn the British and Germans of that sector) lays down its arms; ". . . by simply declining to make an attack, one single French regiment stopped us all," says a runner. The halt is temporary, but the corporal's point is made for all time. The army chiefs see to it that war is resumed—"For six thousand years we labored under the delusion that the only way to stop a war was to get together more regiments and battalions than the enemy could, or vice versa. . ." (75)[1]—the corporal and his commanding general are shot, victory comes, and with it the placing of the unknown soldiers in their

---

[1] All page references given in the text are to *A Fable*.

tombs. With skill and intense irony, Faulkner sees to it that his corporal lies under the Arc de Triomphe.

Upon the frame of that week in May—Monday through the following Sunday—Faulkner has organized his story. But to say this is to give no indication whatever of its fantastic scope. His aim is to show the impact of these events upon a huge number and wide variety of human beings: a Negro preacher from Mississippi, a young British Jew in the R.A.F., a French priest, the American doughboys assigned to shoot the French general, the half-sisters and wife of the condemned corporal, his father the General of the Western Forces, an English horse groom, the German officer who connives in starting the war again, the Middle European squad member who betrays the corporal. Not only this. We learn much about the life of each of these people, and of all the main characters, prior to the fatal week —the events which brought each one where he could be touched or moved or destroyed. The Faulkner flashback has never worked so well as it does in some instances here, notably in the case of the groom, the Rev. Sutterfield and their three-legged race horse, and in the life story of the old General. And more. Faulkner's genius at the epiphany—the complete moment, evoked in truth and dazzling in implication—is everywhere present. Aside from the now-famous described moment of the sunset gun early in the novel, here are the armies after the firing ceases. "So he knew at least where they would be, the whole p. c. of them—colonel, adjutant, sergeant-major, and the telephonist with his temporarily spliced and extended line—topside too, crouching behind the parapet, staring through periscopes across the ruined and silent emptiness at the opposite line, where their opposite German numbers would be crouching also behind a parapet, gazing too through periscopes across that vernal desolation, that silence, expectant too, alerted and amazed" (208). The whole novel is, even more than usually in Faulkner, a carefully organized series of such moments, such flashes of intuition and poetic visions, of movements in time which catch the reader unaware and force him to see the present anew in terms of the past.

Nor is that all. *A Fable* is perhaps first and foremost a commentary on Christ and His message. The days of the cease-fire are the days of the Passion; Christian parallels are myriad and explicit, from the corporal and his twelve disciples (one betrays, one denies thrice) to the Last Supper, the death between thieves and a special kind of Resurrection. The corporal's mother is seen as a vision of Mary, his sisters as Martha and Mary, his wife as Mary Magdalene. It is the old General, the corporal's unproclaimed father, who tempts him (from the height of the Old Citadel) with freedom in the world. More shadowy, but still meaningful on a symbolical level are the John the Baptist groom-sentry, the General Gragnon-Pilate, and the St. Paul-runner, who believes yet never sees his Lord. Many exact ties can be found; many more are suggested and possible. Almost all function in the best way of symbols—to enrich and deepen, without intruding upon, the contemporary story. Delmore Schwartz offers an excellent analogy for the Christian parallels: "The peculiar way in which the Gospel pattern functions can perhaps best be suggested by a metaphor: it is as if, during a play, the actors were seen at recurrent, important moments, varying in length and meaning, in a lighting which like an X-ray machine showed their bone structure, brain, and heart in black, beneath and together with their ordinary visual appearance."[2] Himself a poet, Schwartz perceives better than most critics who have yet written about *A Fable* the true nature of the novel. It is about war ("man's deathless folly"), against war if you will, about the army, religion, politics, and history—but primarily it is an extended incantation about mankind: man in diversity and scope, in sin and goodness. "The real subject is: are human beings worthy of supreme nobility? . . .Thus the chief reason for the Gospel parallel . . . is that the Gospel story represents the kind of being who must exist if any aspiration is to be worthy of realization."[3]

The concern of *A Fable* is man, all kinds of man, in all aspects. It is not by chance that the Nobel Prize speech, virtually intact, appears at the climax of the novel, in the mouth of the General as he offers freedom to his son. Nor is it by chance that the Rev. Tobe Sutterfield, like Dilsey and the host of other Negroes in Faulkner who endure and prevail, says the key words. A lawyer asks him,

> 'Are you an ordained minister?'
> 'I dont know. I bears witness.'
> 'To what? God?'
> 'To man. God dont need me. I bears witness to Him of course, but my main witness is to man.'
> 'The most damning thing man could suffer would be a valid witness before God.'
> 'You're wrong there,' the Negro said. 'Man is full of sin and nature, and all he does dont bear looking at, and a heap of what he says is a shame and mawkery. But cant no witness hurt him . . . .'
> (180)

In another Faulkner novel deeply etched by the Christian story, *Light in*

---

[2] Delmore Schwartz, "*A Fable,*" *Perspectives,* X (1955), 127.
[3] Schwartz, "*A Fable,*" pp. 127, 136.

August,[4] Gail Hightower sighs at the news of Joe Christmas' capture, "Poor man. Poor mankind." He expresses a compassion central to all of Faulkner, but more often felt than stated. Tobe Sutterfield is more explicit. "Evil is a part of man, evil and sin and cowardice, the same as repentance and being brave. You got to believe in all of them, or believe in none of them. Believe that man is capable of all of them, or he aint capable of none" (203).

A Fable aims to show all of these capabilities in man, and to prove by an evocation of the first Son of Man that mankind is "worthy of supreme nobility." The work is of course a profoundly tragic one, for Faulkner is convinced that any Christ is doomed at any time, but that somehow in that doom lies the salvation of each world to come. The figure of St. Paul, the runner, cries out, dying, at the end of the novel, "I'm not going to die. Never." And in that paradox lies our truth, says Faulkner. Bearing witness to man as it does, *A Fable* consistently focuses upon the infinite capacities for joy and sorrow which lie in us all. It is important that in this story of a Son of Man, the miracles, the resurrection remain equivocal. Supernatural events are possible, even probable, yet never certain. Faulkner is demonstrating to us how well mankind's own miraculous nature suffices.

Again and again during the novel we feel the human ties, linking unlike people in similar destinies, touching from Mississippi to the Meuse a common bond of man. Central to this one-mankind concept is the long story of the three-legged race horse. Its presence in the novel is puzzling only in a surface way, though its proportion in terms of overall balance is perhaps harder to justify. It is the story of three people in improbably close communion because of a horse: the Rev. Tobe Sutterfield, his twelve-year-old grandson, and an uncouth Cockney groom. Of the horse, Tobe says, "It was the world's horse. The champion. No, that's wrong too. Things belong to it, not it to things. Things and people both" (150). Three men unite in this belonging to the horse—to an ideal—and accomplish miracles. It is a communion, a shared passion, of which Faulkner as narrator says, ". . .which was why Eve and the Snake and Mary and the Lamb and Ahab and the Whale and Androcles and Balzac's African deserter, and all the celestial zoology of horse and goat and swan and bull, were the firmament of man's history instead of the mere rubble of his past" (161). In the magic of this camaraderie, the groom finds a cause, which he later replaces with his life lottery hold upon the troops of his regiment. This in turn, and with profound upheaval, he gives up for the corporal's cause, no sooner finding his

---

[4] For a detailed analysis of Christian symbols in this novel see Beekman W. Cottrell, "Christian Symbols in *Light in August*," *Modern Fiction Studies*, II (1956-57), 207-213.

life thereby than losing it. It is mankind's great gift to be able to unite and believe and act, and the novel paeans these abilities from the farthest corners of Faulkner's imagination.

Full of the realization of mankind's glorious multiplicity, Faulkner offers his incantatory tale of awe and awareness. Once again he affirms that there can be no truth about a person without his history, no event in time without its past, and often its future as well. Those who perceive best the simple complexity of life, and the complex simplicity, are the suffering and the weak (the Negro preacher, the simple-minded Marya). The innate reaction, no matter how terrifying it appears, is true and strong. Intellectualization is wicked or weak, and so the General loses his battle when the corporal, with innate truthfulness, says, "Don't be afraid. . . . There's nothing to be afraid of. Nothing worth it." He thus seizes the very core of the General's intellectually brilliant if long-winded rationale (Nobel-prizewinning though it be) and wins. If Faulkner, here speaking through the corporal, is a moralist at all he is surely not a doggedly logical theologian. His is a pure faith, and basically a simple one.

To see more clearly the essence of the cosmic novel, it may be instructive to consider briefly another novel built upon the same premise, using the Christ-returned theme and also published (in English) in 1954. It is Nikos Kazantzakis' *The Greek Passion*, but his version of the idea is better expressed in the original Greek title, *Christ Recrucified*. In a Greek village under Turkish rule, the Passion play which is given every seven years is being cast. The parts are in the main justly set—the village prostitute is to play the Magdalene, the village schemer and bully, Judas. A shepherd named Manolios is to portray Jesus. They are all given a year to live with their parts, to consecrate themselves. This is very precisely what happens, as they begin to act their biblical characters in a contemporary crisis. Manolios is so truly imbued with Christlike spirit that he comes to represent the real Jesus to his "disciples" in time of need. He dies for the cause of Greek humanity, under the rule of a power very like that of the Roman empire over Judea.

Yet at least in its English version, *The Greek Passion* is not cosmic in the way of *A Fable*. (Kazantzakis gave his world vision in his last work, *The Odyssey: A Modern Sequel*.) Modern Greeks feel that Kazantzakis has everywhere in his work revitalized their language and many call this vitality his major power. Judged purely as story, *The Greek Passion* is a strong and cleverly integrated realistic novel in which the two levels work together as one, the Gospel parallel constantly illuminating the modern Greek events.

The peasants feel very close to Christ and His life, and their responses are very much in the framework of their known realities. Manolios himself is in tune with Jesus—the miracles and the simple parables and the wandering life of preaching. World dominion and power, complexities of church and state, and the scheming of Pharisees are beyond him or the confines of this novel. In thoroughly natural ways the dual story unfolds. The novel is not the less able for that, but it is deliberately limited to *a* time, *a* place, and a parochial, theological view. Working in this confine, Kazantzakis offers a rich parable himself, but not a world-time fable. He shows what one time and one specific place would do to a returning Jesus, and no more. What emerges is powerful and sufficient. At its heart, *The Greek Passion* takes the same position as Jesus did—and as *A Fable* does.

> Manolios placed his hand on the knee of priest Fotis, who absorbed in his meditations, said nothing.
> "How ought we to love God, Father?" he asked in a whisper.
> "By loving men, my son."
> "And how ought we to love men?"
> "By trying to guide them along the right path."
> "And what is the right path?"
> "The one that rises."[5]

Faulkner is obviously trying for more than a portrait of this simple faith. He too is showing that on the front in 1918 Christ would be recrucified, and the execution justified by all the powers that be. But he steps monumentally beyond and above—out to the whole world of possibility in that or any act of crucifixion, down to the almost unreachable depths of soul which can call it forth, or judge it, or merely know it in deepest anguish. Perhaps *The Greek Passion* is strictly speaking the better novel. In form it is balanced and complete; in conception it is careful and true; in rendering it is believable and real. One reads it and thinks, "How sad, and how true!" With *A Fable*, however, the word *greatness* becomes possible. One reads it and says, "How strange—sad—profound—awesome—mysterious!" One might also very well read it and say, "How turgid and how contrived—" But one cannot let it go at that with this Faulkner. The other side of turgid is dense and brilliant; other words for *contrived* are *formed* and *shaped*. *A Fable* may irk and worry and puzzle. It also very certainly strikes deep into the imagination and emotions, offering new and unexpected or shocking views of life in a way that the more conventional *Greek Passion*, straightforwardly organized and unexceptionable in style, never tries to do. Perhaps it is the

---

[5] Nikos Kazantzakis, *The Greek Passion* (New York, 1954), p. 296.

eternal confrontation of the rough diamond and the brightly polished ruby.

The rough surfaces of *A Fable* have caused more anguish among readers than would seem justified. Perhaps it is only that these show most clearly on a first reading. (One of the major handicaps of the cosmic novel is that it never shows even the half of its riches on first acquaintance.) There are pages of rhetoric, surely, and paragraphs of compounded, exact, yet lifeless generalities. Many of these lack the intensity which would lend validity to such personal statements by a writer. Neither the high tone of incantation nor the presumption that the whole is indeed a fable, spun out by Sage Faulkner from an Oxford, Mississippi, rocking chair, can negate such flaws. Most damaging of all, as one compares *A Fable* to earlier Faulkner novels, is the problem which is here perceptively summarized by Andrew Lytle: ". . . I would say that the author . . . has used his rhetorical gifts to report the action instead of using the rhetoric, as previously, to extend the meaning of the action's violence, thus depriving himself of that extra dimension which his subject needs for its fullest rendition."[6]

Further, the language is too often inconsistent, being in the main British-oriented and erudite, but every now and again slipping into the excessively colloquial and trite ("would notice it without they chanced," or "I wasn't but nine then and Marya eleven" or "working like a beaver, like the very proverbial Trojan, to compensate for his own inability to say no to a woman's tears"). Faulkner has never forced his people, Yoknapatawpha or otherwise, to speak their own language. They start to, he shifts into his own splendid gear, and we benefit from the double level. So it is here with Marthe or the corporal. Faulkner gives us in his own poetic rhythms their inchoate ideas, and it is not surprising that the General and Marya, mentally "light," speak alike on the page. Only Sutterfield and the soldiers keep to their colloquial ways, and even here Faulkner gives us the race horse story filtered through his own magically reflective prose. It is simply too bad that there are lapses, and that the nine years of writing *A Fable* could not have achieved a more consistently interesting, less persistently devious and sometimes more accurately evocative surface.

Once beneath that surface, however, few can cavil. The structure of *A Fable* is monumental, detailed and tremendously effective. It assures that even surface distractions will be no more than noticed after the mid-point. The story is interesting and gathers force until the climax of the corporal's debate with the General. It then tightens into the inevitable tragedy, falls

---

6 Andrew Lytle, "The Son of Man: He will Prevail," *The Sewanee Review*, LXIII (1955), 135.

off to, say, quietude and ends with a bitter, ironic coda called "Tomorrow." The structure is classical, beginning *in medias res* with Wednesday and the arrival of the condemned squad at the prison. Then it returns to how and why, moving forward again through Wednesday and on to the Friday firing squad with its Saturday and Sunday aftermath.

The novel's structure is also operatic, with scenes of light and dark, marvelous movement of crowds (which in Faulkner often take on real life of their own), monologue-arias, and violent climaxes. The best scenes—the sentry and the runner on the firestep, the Citadel debate, the death of General Gragnon, the return of the crippled runner to Marthe's farm, the final tableau at the Arc de Triomphe—rank with the very best of Faulkner's vital work. Through them all, now muted, now forceful, flows the intermittent and powerful beauty of his descriptive prose:

> . . . no longer a starred, solitary man in a staff car behind a French battle-front, but a solitary boy lying on his stomach on a stone wall outside the Pyrenean village where, for all any records stated or knowledge remembered, he had been born an orphan; listening now to the same cicada chirring and buzzing in the tangle of cordite-blasted weeds beyond the escarpment landmarked since last winter by the skeleton tail of a crashed German aeroplane. Then he heard the lark too, high and invisible, almost liquid but not quite, like four small gold coins dropped without haste into a cup of soft silver, he and the driver staring at each other until he said, loud and harsh: 'Drive on!'—moving on again; and sure enough, there was the lark again, incredible and serene, and then again the unbearable golden silence, so that he wanted to clap his hands to his ears, bury his head, until at last the lark once more relieved it. (37)

Full as the novel is of fascinating scene and high rhetoric, the characters also emerge in a typically Faulknerian way. We see them in sudden illuminations, not in steady development, but we nonetheless come to understand and know them. Creation of a "good" person in fiction is difficult, as witness even the failures of John Milton. The corporal here is almost equal to his taxing role—not quite. We believe in him, but wish for more radiance, more force. Not so the old General or his batman; they are fully alive, as are Marthe and Marya, Tobe Sutterfield, the groom, the young British flyer, and, at the last, the sentry. Others are obviously meant for half-portraits. Should we ask more of a fable, or can a writer, so neatly titular, absolve himself to some degree of what many would call the novelist's perennial requirement?

"It has the diffused moral glow of affirmation that writers of talent seem bound to hanker after sooner or later," cries V. S. Pritchett, more in sorrow than in anger.[7] Andrew Lytle adds, "The medium of a craft is always waxen; it is the limits of form which give it flight. It was Daedalus, who did not forget the limits of his craft, who kept his course."[8]

Thus do many informed readers feel about two of the most prominent characteristics of this or any cosmic novel: moral conviction and experimental or irregular form. Pritchett's point is the more damaging, for one may indeed question whether the essay, and not the novel, is not the proper place for prosaic moral or ethical conclusions. But though Daedalus may have kept his course, not forgetting the limits of his craft, it is more often the gloriously fated Icarus whom we remember, whose daring and imagination and high soaring compensate for his ultimate fall. Does the aim of such a cosmic novel as *A Fable* justify its frequent breaks with dramatic presentation and conventional form? Are *Madame Bovary* and *By Love Possessed* more masterful for being conventionally rendered? The only real answers lie with the reader and his preferences—perhaps with the limits of his aesthetic tolerance. Examined closely, however, *A Fable* has at base a surprisingly traditional structure and in that respect is soundly effective; it simply tries to hold more, to be of greater density than the usual novel, bringing to mind *Ulysses* more strongly than any other contemporary work of fiction.

Fictional density demands close attention, and it is again characteristic of such cosmic novels as *A Fable* that they open themselves more fully with each reading. Faulkner's novel, moreover, does the most that can perhaps ever be asked of a cosmic attempt: its basic story and characters are clear and in large measure interesting at the first reading. Complex structure made plain, symbol, shades of tone and color, detail, and wide implication quite naturally emerge only with repeated readings.

There can and should be no rapid judgments for any cosmic novel, and *A Fable* is only now beginning to be understood and savored. The passage of time continues to reveal more fully great cosmic works like *King Lear* and *The Tempest*, *The Brothers Karamazov*, *Pierre* and *Ulysses*. However, there are many to whom any cosmic attempt will never appeal, no matter what its rewards. Perhaps for most readers the necessary efforts of search and puzzle, of being now confused, now overwhelmed, the irritations of disproportion, lecture, musing, direct address and unrelated experiment can never result in satisfaction. Perhaps they are right, and surely their judgments are everywhere soundly defended.

---

[7] V. S. Pritchett, "Time Frozen," *Partisan Review*, XXI (1954), 551.
[8] Lytle, "The Son of Man," p.137.

But it is in complexity and richness, in daring and density, in depth and chiaroscuro, in disproportion and the fresh perception that such masterpieces as *A Fable* have their essence. From such qualities they also, over the years, lose—or gain—their strength.

THAT NOT IMPOSSIBLE HE

FAULKNER'S THIRD-PERSON NARRATOR

JOHN A. HART

FAULKNER'S INTEREST IN TECHNIQUE has led him to try many different forms of narration: sequences of simultaneous events, as in *Mosquitoes*; first-person narrative as in *The Hamlet* and *The Unvanquished*; multiple narrators as in *As I Lay Dying*; dialogue and stage direction as in *Requiem for a Nun*; the omniscient author as in *Old Man*. Another Faulknerian form of narration has much in common with two other forms: with the form to which Henry James has given the name *central intelligence* and with the stream-of-consciousness technique. In James's form, one character, who is consistently referred to in the third person, in general narrates the story as he sees and understands it, with all the limitations and all the perceptions of the narrator's mind. But James, and many others, take advantage of the third-person reference to formalize the description of this character and to narrate his actions where necessary or convenient from outside this character's mind. Faulkner, in contrast, tends to forego this narrative privilege and to confine himself simply to having his narrator see and describe and interpret only what his own mind and senses take in of the action. Faulkner never gives a view of him from the outside. On the other hand, Faulkner (in this form of narration) does not give the fragmented impressions of the mind that are characteristic of the stream-of-consciousness technique. Faulkner's form uses words—"he had heard," "it would seem to him," "he realized," for instance—which have the effect of removing the reader to a certain distance from the thought or impression itself. The form also organizes and stylizes the thought so that it is presented more or less logically rather than in fragmented form. It is as if one person, the narrator, were talking about another person's thoughts, but being limited exactly to that person's view and in fact taking a view identical with it. I will call this form of narration by a short-hand term, third-person narrator, and will examine its use in two of Faulkner's best stories, "The Bear" and *Intruder in the Dust*, a use which contributes substantially to the meaning of each.

2

In "The Bear," Faulkner pays at least lip service to the conventional technique of the central intelligence by using the noun *boy* to refer to his main figure Ike McCaslin whenever a critical confusion might arise if he were to use the pronoun *he*. Thus, at the climax of Part III, we read:

> "No!" Boon said, "No!"
> "Tell the truth," McCaslin [Ike's cousin] said. "I would have done it if he had asked me to." Then the boy moved. He was between them, facing McCaslin; the water felt as if it had burst and sprung not from his eyes alone but from his whole face, like sweat. (254)[1]

Here Faulkner inserts *the boy* instead of *he* to keep the reader from attributing the action of the sentence to Ike's cousin. The meaning, it is true, would eventually have become clear, because the words "He was between them, facing McCaslin" indicate that there are three people involved, that *them* must mean Boon and McCaslin, and that the third must be Ike. This conviction is reinforced by *felt* in the second half of the sentence, since throughout the story otherwise undirected feelings and thoughts are always Ike's. But if *he* were used as the subject of *moved*, the reader could not have identified *he* until after he had already misconstrued the sentence. Hence, at this moment of exciting action, Faulkner uses *boy* to prevent confusion in the reader. More often, however, the author simply uses *he*. In fact, the first reference to Ike made in the story reads: "He was sixteen," a statement which Malcolm Cowley in the *Portable Faulkner* finds it wise to emend to "Ike McCaslin was sixteen." After this initial reference, Faulkner usually employs the pronoun *he*, except in special situations. Whether Faulkner uses noun or pronoun, however, the point of view is always Ike's; and in this sense Ike is the narrator of the story, even though the third person is used throughout.

What is important here is what Faulkner achieves by using the third-person narrator. Soon after the beginning of the story, we see the scene as if

---

1 References given in the text in Part 2 are to *Go Down, Moses*.

it emanated from inside the boy's mind: "For six years now he had heard the best of all talking" (191). And this sentence is followed by two sentences which describe the subjects talked about, the wilderness and hunting, and a third which describes the presence of a bottle during the talking and the narrator's reaction to the alcohol in it. In these three sentences the author establishes the narrator's turn of mind and convictions and the theme of the story he is about to tell. Of the liquor he says, "it would seem to him that those fine fierce instants of heart and brain and courage and wiliness and speed were concentrated and distilled into that brown liquor which not women, not boys and children, but only hunters drank, drinking not of the blood they spilled but some condensation of the wild immortal spirit" (192). The drinking then is a rite which accompanies the talking and gives special meaning to it. He is able to feel and reflect the sanctity of the rite, even though as a child he is not yet a celebrant of it.

He shares also with his fellow hunters a vision of the meaning of hunting and of the wilderness. Hunting is "the ancient and unremitting contest according to the ancient and immitigable rules which voided all regrets and brooked no quarter" (192). This view explains why, although neither he nor Sam Fathers, his mentor, will kill the bear when they have a chance, they go through all the motions of hunting the bear every season; why they know that the bear will eventually be killed; and why Sam himself can train the dog which will help bring the bear to his doom. The hunt, the contest, is always there, making its legitimate claims on men, dogs, bear, and deer, part of the natural law of the wilderness; and Ike from beginning to end accepts this view. It is his awareness and his comprehension of the contest that makes thrilling the part in which he leaves his gun, watch, and compass behind to seek out the bear, the part in which the great dog Lion is brought under control to give the odds to the hunters, and the part in which Boon and Lion finally bring down old Ben.

And his initial description of the wilderness reflects the other hunters' awe and wonder: "[The talking] was of the wilderness, the big woods, bigger and older than any recorded document:—of white man fatuous enough to believe he had bought any fragment of it, of Indian ruthless enough to pretend that any fragment of it had been his to convey" (191). For the other hunters, the attitude is expressed in inarticulate, never clearly understood actions: Major de Spain refuses to return to the wilderness after Old Ben has been hunted down; Sam Fathers gives up living when the bear dies; Ike's cousin McCaslin gives him a shotgun and old General Compson's compass as if he were the sole heir of those who had hunted and were gone; Boon, least able to understand of them all, loses any sense of the significance and dignity of the hunt by the end of the story. Ike is one of them: he catches their feelings, he reflects their views and attitudes. As such, he belongs with them and among them, where the third-person form tends to place him, as the first-person form would tend not to. In this sense, the third-person narrator is appropriate for the story.

At the same time, Ike's vision of the wilderness, born out of the others', goes far beyond theirs. For he sees the relationship between the wilderness— independent of the claims of men, superior to their petty greeds, aloof from their fears, quarrels, and meannesses—and the rest of the land, which ought to be equally free of the claims of men. And he sees the relationship between the wilderness and the dignity and freedom of man, who ought to be free of the institution of slavery and any other kind of racial or economic or political domination of one man by another. The evil is possession, the idea that a man owns wilderness or cultivated land or the person or services of other men.

Some of the others have an inkling of this idea but are corrupted by their own desires. Boon, the simple-minded, who loves and grieves bitterly for the great untamed dog Lion and whose wants and joys are confined almost exclusively to hunting and drinking, is reduced at the end to shouting at Ike: "Dont touch a one of them! They're mine!" (331), meaning only a treeful of squirrels. Major de Spain, who is described at the beginning as "knowing better," leases his legal share of the wilderness to a lumber company, thereby showing his willingness to allow the woods to be destroyed though he is not willing to be witness to the effects of his betrayal. McCaslin Edmonds, without any tendency to destroy at all or to seek possession for himself, is yet unable to see how Ike can reject the land and the possessions so laboriously acquired by his grandfather. Only Sam Fathers, who has suffered as slave and servant all his life and who has left the land and his place in the world to return to the wilderness, would understand Ike's complete vision: as Ike puts it, "Sam Fathers set me free" (300).

But the narrator is not merely a participant in the feelings of all the others nor a man whose vision extends beyond the others', but also a person whose whole lifespan is available to him for whatever understanding it can give him. For this is not a story that takes place exclusively at the time Ike is sixteen. It is also his story at ten and thirteen, twenty-one and seventeen; and earlier than any of these: "[The bear] loomed and towered in his dreams before he even saw the unaxed woods" (193); and later than any of these: "later, years later, after he had grown to a man and had seen the sea" (195); and again, "he would own and shoot [his new gun] for almost seventy years" (205). Other combinations of past, present, and future are also presented here: he saw the wilderness "as it seemed to him later he always saw it or at least always remembered it" (194); "It seemed to him that at the age of ten he was witnessing his own birth. It was not even strange to him. He had experienced it all before, and not merely in dreams" (195-196); "he knew only that for the first time he realised that the bear which had run in his listening and loomed in his dreams since before he could remember and which therefore must have existed in the listening and the dreams of his cousin and Major de Spain and even old General Compson before they began to remember in their turn, was a mortal animal" (200-201).

This freedom to range at will through the whole of the narrator's life sometimes permits Ike to be both a young man and an old man at the same time. For instance, he accurately reads Sam Fathers' reaction to the discovery that the hunters are about to find the powerful dog which will run down Old Ben:

> There was something in Sam's face now. It was neither exultation nor joy nor hope. Later, a man, the boy realised what it had been, and that Sam had known all the time what had made the tracks and what had torn the throat out of the doe in the spring and killed the fawn. It had been foreknowledge in Sam's face that morning. *And he was glad,* he told himself. *He was old. He had no children, no people, none of his blood anywhere above earth that he would ever meet again. And even if he were to, he could not have touched it, spoken to it, because for seventy years now he had had to be a negro. It was almost over now and he was glad.* (214-215)

Two things are noticeable about this passage. First, Ike the boy, along with all the others, is unable to interpret Sam's look. Second, Ike the man does know what the look meant and even knows what Sam was thinking, which then becomes the words he imagines Sam as saying in the present scene. Soon afterwards, Ike wonders about Sam's feelings when Boon takes complete charge of the dog, since the animal rightfully belongs to Sam. "Then he became a man and he knew that too. It had been all right. That was the way it should have been. Sam was the chief, the prince; Boon, the plebeian, was his huntsman. Boon should have nursed the dogs" (222).

With this shifting back and forth in time, Faulkner is able to have his cake and eat it too. He can maintain the freshness and immediacy of the boy's experience; yet at the same time he can have an older and wiser Ike McCaslin give us the thoughts of any of the other characters where they are useful and interpret the events in the light of maturer experience and knowledge.

The contribution made by the form of narration in accomplishing this legerdemain seems fairly clear if we consider alternative forms. The first-person narrative would retain the immediacy but involve the writer in a much more conscious treatment of the differences between the earlier and later Ike McCaslin, much as we find done in Warren's *All the King's Men*, where the difference between the present and the past is distinguished carefully, though occasionally with some awkwardness. The omniscient-author technique, of course, would sacrifice the immediacy and excitement of the other two devices.

If this form of narration were simply clever, the description of it would be interesting but scarcely relevant. Actually, the meaning of the story depends upon the tension between the successive responses of young Ike and the reflections upon those responses by an older Ike. Young Ike *feels* the kinship of Sam Fathers, of the bear, of the wilderness; he *feels* the malignancy of the dog, the antagonism to Boon, the unfailing contest between hunter and hunted; he *feels* too the difference between the legitimate though fatal struggle of the hunt and the possessiveness of the men who would destroy the wilderness for their own advantage. Then as a young adult he is old enough to "say it," to articulate his repudiation of his inheritance, of slavery, of the destruction of either land or person by possessive man. His emotions at this time do not entirely correspond to his intellectual convictions, however, as we see when he yields, momentarily at least, in passion to his wife's longing to possess the land he has repudiated. Overall, the old man, the Ike of seventy and more, reflects upon and contemplates the life that the boy and the young man have known, bringing to the scene both feeling and understanding never really combined in either of the other two. Thus the choice of the narrative form makes a major contribution to the success of the story.

3

In *Intruder in the Dust*, Chick Mallison occupies as narrator the same position that Ike McCaslin does in "The Bear." But everything now emanates from the narrator's mind; Faulkner no longer permits himself the luxury of inserting a clarifying noun to keep the references to person straight.

At first, Faulkner's determination not to compromise with the conventional use of the central intelligence merely annoys the reader. The first sentence says that everyone knew that Lucas Beauchamp had killed a white man; the second sentence says, "He was there, waiting" (3).[2] The logic of English grammar would make *He* refer to Lucas; but it does not, it refers to Chick, the narrator. The chances are strong that any given *he*, *his*, or *him* will refer to Chick; the irritation arises out of the fact that the reader can not depend on it. For instance, the first chapter contains the following passage, for which I have supplied the pronoun references (as I read them):

> "What's that for?" the man [Lucas] said, not even moving, not even tilting his [Lucas's] face downward to look at what was on his [Chick's] palm: for another eternity and only the hot dead moveless blood until at last it ran to rage so that at least he [Chick] could bear the shame: and [Chick] watched his [Chick's] palm turn over not flinging the coins but spurning them downward ringing onto the bare floor, bouncing and one of the nickels even rolling away in a long swooping curve with a dry minute sound like the scurry of a small mouse: and then his [Lucas's] voice:
>   "Pick it up!" (15-16)

It is a minor irritation, of course; a careful rereading will invariably reconstruct the references. But the method of narration would seem to ask for justification, if for no other reason than to counterbalance the reader's irritation, especially when he realizes that a first-person narration might have been substituted, thereby making his reading job easier.

If we look for likenesses to the form of narration in "The Bear," we see, but only rarely, that Chick, like Ike, looks upon the events he is participating in from an older point of view: "But the smell meant nothing now or yet; it was still an hour yet before the thing would happen and it would be four years more before he would realise the extent of its ramifications and what it had done to him and he would be a man grown before he would realise, admit that he had accepted it" (11). Instances like this are important to the story because they show that the awakening taking place at the present in Chick's mind will not be reversed.

But that purpose is clearly not the major reason for using this form of narration in *Intruder in the Dust*. Here the primary purpose is obviously to reveal the process of awakening that the narrator experiences exactly as the mind would know and express it. Every characteristic of Chick's mind is made an inherent part of the narration. We see in operation, for instance, his memory: ". . . the cryptic three-toed prints of chickens like (remembering it now at sixteen) a terrain in miniature . . ." (8-9). Or the impreciseness of

---

2 References given in the text in Part 3 are to *Intruder in the Dust*.

his thought: ". . . a face which in his estimation might have been under fifty or even forty except for the hat and the eyes . . ." (6). Or his way of rationalizing: ". . . still telling himself this even after he knew that the true reason was . . ." (8). Or the way he discovers something: ". . . he did pause long enough to look at her because he was about to remember something else his uncle had told him about or at least in regard to Lucas Beauchamp, and looking at her he realised for the first time how old the man actually was, must be . . ." (10). Or the way he sees: ". . . a hall dim even almost dark after the bright outdoors . . ." (9).

In addition to these mental characteristics, the activity of the unconscious is captured very convincingly. For example, at Chick's first meeting with Lucas, he is determined, he believes, not to follow Lucas into his house, but when he gets to the path, he not only follows him but realizes that he was going to follow him all along, that there was no way he could have resisted the older man's insistence. Again, Chick has various struggles to control his conscious mind: to go to sleep the first night Lucas is arrested, to stay awake after his all-night experience of grave-digging, or to contend with the effects of coffee: "He still needed to doze only now he couldn't; the desire to sleep was there but it was wakefulness now he would have to combat and abate" (133). He also has daydreams: after Lucas has been arrested, of riding Highboy miles and miles away from "Jefferson and nigger murderers" (67); after the mob discovers Lucas is innocent, of Miss Habersham driving miles and miles into the next county because she is caught in the crush of vehicles leaving town. The shadowy uncertainty of his memory is also illustrated: "But he couldn't think what it was his uncle had said or told him and then he forgot that he had remembered even the having been told" (10).

These illustrations suggest the detail and the care with which Faulkner reveals the thought processes of his narrator. They could, of course, be multiplied many times, for the texture of the story is laced with the workings of Chick's mind. The operation of that mind is most clearly revealed in the first two chapters, which deal with three subjects primarily: relations between Chick and Lucas preliminary to the present action; Chick's mental turmoil when he learns that Lucas is alleged to be a murderer; and his awareness and reaction when he realizes that the atmosphere of the town has changed at the news.

From that point on, there is an action to describe, and the thickness of the texture can be somewhat attenuated whenever the necessity arises. What is described is always observed by Chick, but there is not as much consistent attention given to the working of his mind. For instance,

> They were going quite fast now, faster than he could ever re-member his uncle driving, out the long road where he had ridden last night on the horse but in daylight now, morning's bland in-effable May; now he could see the white bursts of dogwood in the hedgerows marking the old section-line surveys or standing like nuns in the cloistral patches and bands of greening woods and the pink and white of peach and pear and the pinkwhite of the first apple trees in the orchards which last night he had only smelled: and al-ways beyond and around them the enduring land. (146)

The details of the story and the picture of the other characters are taken care of in this way primarily. But they are helped along by two other charac-teristics of Faulkner's method here. One of these is the knack Chick has of suggesting the effect on the townspeople of the murder and arrest, not by saying what it is, but by describing the way the town has looked on a routine day and noting the change. On Sunday evening the streets are customarily filled with casually walking church goers; *this* Sunday night they are de-serted. Monday morning usually finds buses taking children to school, farmers driving in to do their marketing; *this* Monday the vehicles are there but they contain the mob come to witness the lynching.

The second of these characteristics consists of Chick's own fine quali-ties of observation, perception, and sensitivity. He thinks the same thoughts that his uncle proceeds to utter, he perceives that his father's gruff speech to him is actually envy and admiration, he recognizes that Lucas's eyes, and later old Gowrie's eyes, reveal grief for the death of a loved one.

The sensitivity has to be acute, the awareness of past and present must be strong, the observation has to be reliable and accurate. For the novel depends greatly upon a clear view of motivation in the other characters. Thus, the response of the mob must be understood by the reader, so that not merely the spoken shouts may be heard, but the emotional undercurrents may be experienced clearly—the restlessness, the ominous quiet, the purpose-ful gathering, and finally the shameful retreat. And the same clarity of view must be given to old Gowrie, the symbol of the ruthless prejudice of Beat Four; and to Sheriff Hampton, who strongly, intelligently, and fearlessly carries out the law, without any indication that he is sympathetic to racial equality; and to Miss Habersham, whose sense of fairness and whose strong affection for Lucas's deceased wife lead her to take part in the grave-digging with Chick; and to Lucas, who quietly but firmly insists on his own rights.

And finally and most importantly, clarity must be given to Gavin Stevens, Chick's enlightened uncle, whose perception and articulateness threaten to dominate the story.

In the depiction of these characters, the third-person form of narration plays a significant part. Before I consider the contribution of the form, however, I should like to elaborate briefly on the distinctions in racial attitude among the characters. The mob and Gowrie, potentially an irresistible force in the novel, are convinced that "niggers" in general, and Lucas in particular, have to be kept in their place. Hampton, the strongest controlling force, remains neutral and insists on law and order. Miss Habersham, a force because she is a woman of vigor and conviction, defies the men and the racial tradition and does her part to save Lucas from injustice. Most of all among these characters, Gavin Stevens sees beyond the narrow prejudices of the townspeople, and his eloquence, high intelligence, and sense of fairness give him influence in the community.

Of these characters Stevens produces the strongest impact on the reader with his vision of the reconciliation of white and Negro on a basis of equality in the future, if enough time is allowed to elapse and if the South is allowed to work out the relationship without interference from outside:

> Someday Lucas Beauchamp can shoot a white man in the back with the same impunity to lynch-rope or gasoline as a white man; in time he will vote anywhen and anywhere a white man can and send his children to the same school anywhere the white man's children go and travel anywhere the white man travels as the white man does it. (155)
> I'm defending Lucas Beauchamp. I'm defending Sambo from the North and East and West—the outlanders who will fling him decades back not merely into injustice but into grief and agony and violence too by forcing on us laws based on the idea that man's injustice to man can be abolished overnight by police. . . . I only say that the injustice is ours, the South's. We must expiate and abolish it ourselves, alone and without help nor even (with thanks) advice. (203-204)

In comparison with these others, Gavin is clearly champion and spokesman of progress. But when we set him alongside his nephew, who is quick to acknowledge his admirable qualities, the picture changes. Gavin, we recall, did not give Lucas a chance to explain what kind of help he wanted, and would not listen to Chick when he tried to explain. To both, his rejection is couched in the familiar assumptions that have been made by all the townspeople and the vocabulary they regularly use.

> Lucas . . . has it ever occurred to you that if you just said mister
> to white people and said it like you meant it, you might not be sitting
> here now? (62)

> So you took your pistol and went to straighten it out. You, a nigger,
> took a pistol and went to rectify a wrong between two white men.
> What did you expect? What else did you expect? (63)

> That's exactly what I would claim myself if I were Lucas—or any
> other Negro murderer for that matter or any ignorant white murderer
> either for the matter of that. (79)

In these comments, Gavin shows no perception either of Lucas or Chick,
but only of the stereotype of both he has constructed or inherited or arrived
at through his "experience" with Negroes and children. Chick also compares
his father's and his uncle's responses to his successful grave-digging exploit,
unfavorably for his uncle: "it was his uncle's abnegant and rhetorical self-
lacerating which was the phony one and his father was gnawing the true
bitter irremediable bone. . ." (133). And it is this disparity between his
uncle's persuasive rhetoric and his genuine convictions that Chick, unwill-
ingly, is critical of: "now he heard for the third time almost exactly what
he had heard twice in twelve hours, and he marvelled again at the paucity,
the really almost standardised meagreness not of individual vocabularies
but of Vocabulary itself, by means of which even man can live in vast droves
and herds even in concrete warrens in comparative amity: even his uncle
too . . ." (80). Hence, despite the closeness of the two, despite all that Chick
has learned from his uncle, they and their views are not at all identical; in
fact, Chick is as far from his uncle as his uncle is from any other character
in the book.

Chick stands alone. His is the one other force of consequence. This force
is expressed only secondarily in the action taken to help Lucas. Primarily,
it is expressed by the activity of that mind of the third-person narrator:
imprecise, flickering, remembering and forgetting, rationalizing, but discovering itself and the world around it; for this activity is what confronts
and defeats all of the other forces in the story. With all its limitation, this
mind is man creating his own thought. It will not allow its native prejudice
to gain the ascendancy; it will not accept without question the standard
words or the stereotyped ideas of its tradition; it will not stand still and
listen to the mob, or a mother's caution, or an uncle's advice. On the contrary,
it works, searchingly and fumblingly but surely and unceasingly, toward a
new attitude which will reconcile the almost irremovable prejudice and the
new growing feeling of respect for the individual no matter what his class-

ification or type. The untenable view of white supremacy held by the mob, and the more "advanced" view of Gavin Stevens that a long period will eliminate the feeling of tension and significant distinction between the races, are both made to look a little foolish because the change intellectualized so pompously by Stevens is occurring, has been fought and won, inside the consciousness of the narrator.

What has been said about Chick's importance as a character is relevant to the use of the third-person narrator in the novel. I pointed out earlier that the thought process is presented to great advantage through this technique. The reader is not seeing the mind from so close a position that he would be tempted to identify with it (as he would if the first person were used). At the same time, no exception is provided under which the author could even momentarily switch to view Chick from the outside. Events are always dealt with through the narrator's mind.

There is another advantage of this form of narration. This has to do with how the other characters are depicted. I said that they had to be seen clearly and that they were. This could not have been done as easily if the first-person narrator had been used because the reader would be too much aware of the narrator's presence and the narrator's bias. But where the third-person narrator is used, we can be led to accept the presence of the author's judgment as well as Chick's because of the illusion that the form creates. Though Chick is alone and apart from his fellow characters in perception, we see him (in the third person) as among them, and we tend to regard their reactions and his reactions on the same plane. This makes it easier for us to accept them as clearly and objectively characterized and to see him as possessing no special wisdom or powers in characterizing them but instead as struggling to solve problems in the same way but with greater success than they.

Thus the third-person narrator becomes important to "The Bear" and *Intruder in the Dust*, but for very different reasons. Both have moved away from James's method of characterizing the narrator from the outside before slipping into his consciousness. In "The Bear," the function of the third-person form of narration is to allow Ike to share with others the experience of the story, and to enable him to interpret his and their reactions to that experience partly because he has stronger perceptions than they and partly because he is allowed a lifetime of experience to base his understanding on. In *Intruder in the Dust*, the function of the third-person form of narration is to display Chick's creative and energetic mind and to portray the other characters clearly and objectively. Though the form is that of the third-person narrator in both, Faulkner fits the form to his purpose and idea and makes it contribute substantially and peculiarly to the meaning of each story.

"THE BEAR"
AND FAULKNER'S MORAL VISION

DURING THE PAST DECADE, the interpretation of Faulkner's fiction has become increasingly dependent upon interpretation of the course his career has taken, especially of the shift that separates the works he published between 1929 and 1940 from those he has published since 1948. The differences between the two groups of works are quite evident. The stark inwardness and dramatic self-sufficiency of the earlier novels contrast plainly with the overt philosophizing and the seemingly didactic use of Christian motifs in the later ones. The world in which the Compsons and Bundrens and Sutpens suffer differs from that in which Gavin Stevens and the old commander moralize. Temple Drake the distraught flapper of *Sanctuary* is not Temple Drake the tortured penitent of *Requiem for a Nun*; Ratliff the wry connoisseur of Snopesism in *The Hamlet* becomes another man viewing askance the progress of a disease in *The Town* and *The Mansion*. Yet evident as these differences are, the nature and significance of the shift are not generally agreed upon; nor is it agreed what bearing the shift has on interpretation of Faulkner's work—whether its moral focus has altered and different outlooks are to be distinguished, or its moral focus has remained the same and the earlier works are now best read in the light of the later.

The most widely held view of this shift seems to run something like this: The works of the earlier period, the "time of genius," are predominantly somber and negative, affirmation being crowded to the peripheries as goodness is perpetually overbalanced by evil and violence. Stirrings toward a

redress of the balance are evident in *The Hamlet*, and "The Bear" heralds
Faulkner's emergence into the downright affirmation of the later works. If
the earlier works are pervaded by an Old Testament gloom, the later are
suffused with New Testament light, "The Bear" representing an annunci-
ation. In the works published after "The Bear," especially in *Requiem for a
Nun* and *A Fable*, Faulkner moves decisively into a modern restatement of
Christian myth and an explicit assertion of Christian values.[1]

   This view of Faulkner's career does not often involve a precise formulation of how and how far his fiction is implicated in Christian values, nor
does it always involve a clear account of the nature of the shift. In any case,
it is a view that needs, I believe, to be challenged, both in its account of
Faulkner's moral vision and in the notions about the shift which follow
from that account. Faulkner's moral vision, it seems to me, clearly invites
formulation in humanistic, not religious terms. His fiction, it must be
granted, is often ambiguous in the values it expresses; no perversity is required to decide that they are Christian values, for it is at least plain that
they are consistent with Christian values. The Christian motifs and Biblical
analogies, however—both covert and overt, early and late—seem to me to
parallel a humanistic vision, to illuminate and reinforce it, but not to transform it into a Christian account of man. They are a part of the structure of
individual works, but they do not determine the essential burden of the
work as a whole. Similarly, I view the shift in Faulkner's work neither as a
changing expression of Christian values, at first tentative or submerged and
later brought into the open, nor as a revision of moral outlook from a notion
that most men are doomed to a notion that most may be saved. The values
expressed in his works seem quite consistent from first to last. The shift
reflects less a change of emphasis from 'negative values to positive than a
change in the manner of presenting those values, a change from the dramatic
and implicit to the rhetorical and explicit.[2]

   These considerations have an obvious relevance to a reading of "The
Bear." It has been rightly recognized by many critics as being crucial to
any interpretation of Faulkner's moral vision, but it will be read differently

---

[1] Among the most persuasive statements of this view are that of Hyatt H. Waggoner
in *William Faulkner: From Jefferson to the World* (Lexington, Ky., 1959), pp. 238-
251; and that of R. W. B. Lewis in "The Hero in the New World: William Faulkner's
'The Bear,'" *Kenyon Review*, 1951, reprinted in *Interpretations of American Literature*, ed. Feidelson and Brodtkorb (New York, 1959), pp. 332-335.

[2] This view of Faulkner agrees, I believe, with that given by Frederick J. Hoffman in
his introduction to *William Faulkner: Three Decades of Criticism*, ed. Hoffman and
Vickery (East Lansing, Mich., 1960), pp. 30-42, and in his *William Faulkner* (New
York, 1961), pp. 8, 106-118.

by critics holding differing views of its relation to the rest of the Faulkner canon. It has been called a "pivotal work" in the shift from Faulkner's earlier work to his later.[3] There are good reasons for so calling it: it exhibits a more direct concern with moral values than the works that precede it; it contains a more explicit use of Biblical parallels; and it possesses an aura of mysticism that does not appear in earlier works. Clearly enough, "The Bear" marks the change in Faulkner's fictional manner, but I question that it marks any more radical change. Rather, it expresses more plainly than any other work the humanistic values consistent throughout his work—values clearly implicit in the best short stories and the great novels of 1929 to 1940, and more explicit, though often less clear, in the novels published since 1948.

2

The structure of "The Bear," notwithstanding the real but over-celebrated difficulty of the narrative, is entirely lucid. Both its coherence and its difficulty arise from its being a record of the consciousness of Isaac McCaslin. The story *is* Ike McCaslin's consciousness for the most part, and the narrative—with its flow of reminiscence and speculation in Faulknerian periods, its abrupt parentheses and digressions, its remote or suspended references, its submerged and implicit meaning—is designed to convey that consciousness with dramatic immediacy. As in others of Faulkner's works, aspects of consciousness are juxtaposed with one another and in turn with action which issues from that consciousness, but the thematic relationships which unite these things are left unspecified. The meaning of the work is defined and its structure elaborated as these relationships are established.

In the case of "The Bear," establishing them is less problematic than in some of Faulkner's other major works, because a single act stands central to the whole story: Ike's repudiation of the legacy that comes to him from his grandfather through his father and uncle, his refusal to take possession of the McCaslin plantation or to benefit from its revenues. That moral act climaxes a process of learning to which everything else in the story is related as preparation, confirmation, or explanation. "The Bear" is a *Bildungsroman*, as is acknowledged in Ike's reflection on "how much it takes to compound a man (Isaac McCaslin for instance) and of the devious intricate choosing yet unerring path that man's (Isaac McCaslin's for instance) spirit takes among all that mass to make him at last what he is to be" (308-309).[4] But the narrative is not that of a traditional *Bildungsroman* such as *Great Expecta-*

---

[3] Lewis, "The Hero,"*Interpretations of American Literature,* p. 333.
[4] All page references given in the text are to *Go Down, Moses.*

tions or *Of Human Bondage* or even *A Portrait of the Artist as a Young Man*. There is no direct presentation in the story of a moment at which Ike formulates his decision for himself, no single moment of full enlightenment; in a sense the story is *entirely* preparation, confirmation, and explanation. The decision is taken not at the end but in the middle, Ike's explanation of it framed by his initiation into the mysteries of the wilderness (Parts I-III and V) and interrupted by his musing excursions into his family's past. The narrative represents not a cumulative sequence of events issuing in discovery and action, but a confluence, a simultaneous awareness of the several strands of his experience that give his decision its distinctive moral content.

The story actually concerns not simply one material legacy but several moral legacies, and the way Ike's mind threads its way among them, accepting and rejecting. The one which is developed at greatest length is that which he receives from Sam Fathers and Old Ben, the story of his boyhood initiation in woodsmanship, his acquisition of a special attitude toward nature, and his last return to the wilderness at the age of eighteen. This legacy he accepts. The second legacy comes from Carothers McCaslin, his grandfather—a heritage of attitudes toward the use of land and men which were held by the man who founded the McCaslin family and plantation. These he rejects. The third legacy is that of his father and uncle, who held attitudes opposed to his grandfather's. These he accepts. The fourth legacy, which he receives from his maternal uncle, Hubert Beauchamp, does not contribute to his decision to repudiate the plantation, but in a humorously ironic way confirms it.

When Ike enters the wilderness at ten for the first of many semi-annual hunts, he begins an apprenticeship and, as it is called in the story, a "novitiate" to Sam Fathers. Sam is not a natural man and noble savage, an innocent unspoiled by civilization, but rather a deeply sophisticated and completely disciplined man. He is the inheritor of the now passing but long-established culture of the Indians who made their life in the Southern forests by their native intelligence and skill. Ike's education at Sam's hands is a literal apprenticeship; Sam instructs him in the arts of finding one's way in the forest, locating game, and hunting safely. But learning the discipline of woodsmanship becomes something like a religious initiation—a test of skill and steadiness in which Ike proves his worthiness to membership in a private society of devotees. The whole matter grows up between Ike and Sam; none of the other hunters shares in it. And the attitudes shared by the old man and the boy remain largely unspoken between them. Ike grasps intuitively from the start that Sam's disciplined life involves not only skill but a reverence for wild nature and a sense of his own dignity as a part of that nature. Ike sets out to realize these values for himself.

The test is of his own devising. On his second visit to the hunting camp Ike resolves, without telling even Sam, to seek out Old Ben, the great bear who has for years outwitted all hunters, and have a look at him. After he searches the forest unsuccessfully for three days, Sam, guessing his purpose, tells him to leave his gun behind and try again. He does so, again unsuccessfully, but before giving up leaves his watch and compass behind on a bush and makes the final and successful attempt. In performing this act, he "relinquished completely" to the wilderness. Out of his desire for contact with the bear—the "epitome and apotheosis of the old, wild life"—he relinquishes all trappings of civilization, all mechanical aids, and braves the wilderness with only his native capacities. He becomes purely a part of nature, seeking to meet Old Ben on his own ground, unsupported and unprotected by anything other than his ability to make his way in the forest. His reward is a sight of Old Ben. Becoming lost, he circles to find his own track into the forest, and failing to find it, pauses "seeing as he sat down on the log the crooked print, the warped indentation in the wet ground which while he looked at it continued to fill with water" (208-209). Looking up, he sees across a glade first his watch and compass, and then also the bear. The moment signifies Ike's acceptance by Old Ben and the wilderness, by nature itself, as allied with them.

This episode smacks of the pathetic fallacy, as indeed do a number of episodes in the account of Ike's novitiate. That account has a mystical tone, for it embodies a view of nature that is pantheistic and sacramental, a suggestion that nature itself is god and that men best seek as nearly as they can to unite themselves with it. Yet no metaphysical position is stated or implied by Ike or Sam. The narrative focuses not on their beliefs but on their attitudes and behavior toward nature, which suggest that it is worthy of reverence, *as if* it were godlike, *as if* it incarnated an ultimate reality. And the narrative touches on their unspoken attitudes toward themselves—Sam's calm assurance that he is at one with the wilderness, Ike's growing self-respect as a woodsman and hunter, a self-respect divorced from all social sources of pride.

Their further behavior confirms and extends their attitude toward nature. In the third year of Ike's hunting, they ambush Old Ben, and Ike's mongrel terrier raises such a yapping that the bear rears at bay against a tree trunk. Though they are so close that they could not miss the shot, neither shoots, and after the bear's escape they tacitly agree that they do not want to kill him, that they prefer to run him as a ritual contact with "the old, wild life" and to spare him in order to prolong the contact. In this they acknowl-edge that hunting is a violation of nature, though an acceptable one—an activity that proceeds by rule, and, by pitting human cunning fairly against animal cunning, brings hunters close to nature. But they wish to spare Old Ben even from this acceptable form of violation, recognizing as they agree not to kill him that "somebody is going to, some day" and that "it must be one of us" (212).

But Sam does better than kill Old Ben himself. He traps a savage wild dog, starves it into obedience, and trains it to hunt. He does not, could not tame the dog—"I don't want him tame." If Old Ben is to die, Sam prefers to see him run down and killed by another wild creature. In Ike's sixteenth year, the dog, Lion, does run down Old Ben. And at the very moment Old Ben dies, Sam collapses on the forest floor. A doctor pronounces the trouble exhaustion; only Ike "knew that Sam too was going to die." And three days later Sam is dead. It is as if he has prepared, consciously engineered his death as he wishes it to be. Knowing that the killing of Old Ben will symbolize the passing of the wilderness, its imminent destruction by civilization, and with it the possibility of his way of life, Sam devises as nearly as he can a sacramental end to the running of the great bear.

When Ike returns at eighteen for a visit to the forest in which he has hunted, he confirms his acceptance of the legacy left him by Sam. He visits the grave where he helped to bury Sam—"the old man born of a Negro slave and a Chickasaw chief who had been his spirit's father if any had, whom he had revered and harkened to and loved and lost and grieved" (326). He observes preparations for the monstrous logging operation which will in actual fact destroy the forest. He rides in on the log-train, and "it was as though the train . . . had brought with it into the doomed wilderness, even before the actual axe, the shadow and portent of the new mill not even finished yet and the rails and ties which were not even laid; and he knew now . . . that after this time he himself, who had had to see it one time other, would return no more" (321). Ike's unvoiced thought is that the logging operation, the destruction of the forest for profit, represents pre-cisely the contrary of the attitudes toward nature that he shared with Sam and still holds himself—Sam's gift. Nature for him is an end, not a means; or, to put it another way, man's proper end is to be a part of nature, not to make of it an instrument of his own purpose.

The moral legacies left to Ike by his grandfather and by his father and uncle are detailed chiefly in a long digression in Part IV of "The Bear"

(261-282). In 1883, his sixteenth year and the same year in which Sam dies, Ike goes secretly one night to the commissary of the McCaslin plantation to look at the ledgers in which the plantation's affairs have been recorded. He never knew his grandfather, and his father and uncle both died in the early years of his childhood. From the brief and often cryptic entries in the ledgers and from hearsay, Ike pieces together what sort of men his progenitors were—as does the reader of "The Bear."

The figure of old Lucius Quintus Carothers McCaslin is dimly and distantly seen both by Ike and by the reader. He was born in Carolina in 1772 and came to Mississippi sometime around the turn of the century to found his plantation. North Mississippi was then a frontier wilderness in which Carothers no doubt cleared and plowed his own portion of land, acquired no one knows exactly how. He brought Negro slaves with him from Carolina to do the labor or help with it, and he later acquired more, enough to bequeath to his twin sons at his death in 1837 twenty-four slaves. Evidently he sought not only a comfortable way of life but grandeur, for at his death a great house built by his slaves was left—"the tremendously-conceived, the almost barnlike edifice, . . . scarcely yet out of embryo, as if even old Carothers McCaslin had paused aghast at the concrete indication of his own vanity's boundless conceiving" (262).

Ike, even knowing no more than these bare facts, might reject Carothers out of reverence for the wilderness that Carothers displaced with a farm and the "tremendous abortive edifice." But the act that fixes his rejection involved not Carothers' relation to the land, but his relations with his slaves. In 1807, the ledger entries reveal, he made the long journey through the wilderness to New Orleans, where he purchased a slave, Eunice, for the high price of $650. In 1809, he married her to Thucydides, a family slave whom he had brought from Carolina, and in 1810 she bore a daughter, Tomey. The repercussions of these acts, outwardly normal for that time and place, occurred years later. On Christmas day, 1832, Eunice drowned in a creek on the plantation, just six months before Tomey, grown but unmarried, gave birth to a child. Ike's Uncle Buddy wrote in the ledger that Eunice drowned herself; he gave no reason, but evidently it concerned her daughter's pregnancy. And in 1837, just after the death of Carothers, Thucydides refused absolutely to accept an unexplained legacy of ten acres of land left him by his master.

Ike guesses the ugly meaning of these facts. Carothers had bought for himself a slave mistress, fathered a daughter upon her, and married her quickly to another slave to give the child a black father. Twenty-three years later, he fathered another child upon his own daughter, and his mistress, as soon as the fact was apparent, killed herself. Upon his death, the Negro foster father refused to accept any compensation for the injury done his family, declining to countenance their suffering in the slightest way, even after the fact. What shocks Ike is his vision of Eunice's suffering, of the violence done her feelings toward Carothers and toward her daughter: "he seemed to see her actually walking into the icy creek on that Christmas day six months before her daughter's and her lover's (*Her first lover's* he thought. *Her first*) child was born, solitary, inflexible, griefless, ceremonial, in formal and succinct repudiation of grief and despair who had already had to repudiate belief and hope" (271). And what shocks him even more is the carelessness with which he imagines his grandfather to have violated his daughter and broken her mother:

> *But there must have been love* he thought. *Some sort of love. Even what he* [Carothers] *would have called love: not just an afternoon's or a night's spittoon.* There was the old man, old, within five years of his life's end, long a widower and, since his sons were not only bachelors but were approaching middleage, lonely in the house and doubtless even bored since his plantation was established now and functioning and there was enough money now, too much of it probably for a man whose vices even apparently remained below his means; there was the girl, husbandless and young, only twenty-three when the child was born: perhaps he had sent for her at first out of loneliness, to have a young voice and movement in the house, summoned her, bade her mother send her each morning to sweep the floors and make the beds and the mother acquiescing since that was probably already understood, already planned . . . that evil and unregenerate old man who could summon, because she was his property, a human being because she was old enough and female, to his widower's house and get a child on her and then dismiss her because she was of an inferior race. . . . (270, 294)

The revelation of his grandfather's incest and miscegenation holds for Ike the essential meaning of the plantation system: it is founded on casual exploitation and violation of men by other men. Rejecting the system, he declines to possess the plantation. Men are no more properly used as instruments than is nature, and Ike, like Thucydides, refuses even after the fact to condone it, to profit from it, to have any part in it. In refusing the legacy of the plantation, Ike repudiates his grandfather's unconcerned violence upon human decency and dignity.

If Ike finds the pattern of an appropriate attitude toward nature in Sam Fathers, he finds the pattern of an appropriate attitude toward men in his father, Theophilus McCaslin (Uncle Buck), and his uncle, Amodeus McCaslin (Uncle Buddy). The pattern is dimmer, but it involves at least the repudiation of slavery and the attempt to remedy its injustice. The twin brothers remained bachelors past sixty, when Uncle Buck married—presumably trapped by Miss Sophonsiba Beauchamp who became Ike's mother. Clearly neither of them had an interest in forwarding a McCaslin dynasty. Equally clearly, neither wished to forward the plantation system. On the very day of their father's death in 1837 they began freeing the slaves he had left to them, evidently holding clear and firm convictions against slavery but having kept silent while their father lived and they could not implement them. They refused to fall in with the ambition their father seems to have had, and also to countenance or use slave labor, moving out of the big unfinished house as soon as their father was buried and "into a one-room log cabin which the two of them built themselves and added other rooms to while they lived in it, refusing to allow any slave to touch any timber of it other than the actual raising into place the logs which two men alone could not handle" (262). As though "long since past any oral intercourse" about slavery, the brothers communicated with each other about the Negroes by exchanging notes written as entries in the commissary ledgers.

Those entries reflect the enlightened attitude Buck and Buddy held toward the Negroes, the code—perhaps unformulated—by which they dealt with them. When the slaves were given their freedom in 1837, it was offered to them but not forced upon them; they were allowed to do with it what they liked. Roscius and Phoebe, the parents of Thucydides, elected to remain on the plantation, and, the ledger entries suggest, they lived there until the end of their lives. The legacy of the ten-acre piece of land was not forced upon Thucydides, nor was the $200 offered him as a substitute by Buck and Buddy. He apparently insisted upon accepting no gift from a white McCaslin, insisted upon working out his worth as a slave before accepting freedom. Buck and Buddy allowed him his conception of his own integrity.

Their tolerance toward the Negroes is amusingly illustrated in the episode of Percival Brownlee, the slave whom Buck unaccountably bought in 1856. No doubt the purchase resulted from mesmeric persuasion by the slave-trader, Nathan B. Forrest, and it was a transaction in which Buck was badly beaten. He expected Brownlee to be of use as a clerk and bookkeeper—perhaps hoping to delegate management of the Negroes' affairs to one of themselves—but soon discovered that he could not read or write. Brownlee proved also totally inept at field work and handling stock, and after his involvement in a mule's broken leg and consequent destruction, he was despairingly freed by the twins. He did not immediately leave the plantation, and Buck and Buddy tolerated his delay. The notes they wrote each other about Brownlee are humorously matter-of-fact and uncomplaining; they accepted being victimized by Forrest, and they betrayed no rancor or vindictiveness toward Brownlee. Their patience is the more remarkable in that Brownlee may have made trouble for them among the Negroes: his incompetence was accompanied by effeminacy and, almost certainly, homosexuality. Uncle Buddy suggested that he remained on the plantation because of homosexual attachments.[5]

A final example of the humane attitude Buck and Buddy held toward the Negroes is their arrangement for the nighttime hours when the Negroes were not at work. During the day, apparently—the matter is not made clear —they expected all the Negroes to contribute to their own maintenance by contributing to the economy of the plantation that supported them. At sundown, however, they herded them in the front door of their sleeping quarters—the unfinished mansion itself "which lacked half its windows and had no hinged back door at all." There was an "unspoken gentlemen's agreement between the two white men and the two dozen black ones that, after the white man had counted them and driven the home-made nail into the front door at sundown, neither of the white men would go around behind the house and look at the back door, provided that all the Negroes were behind the front one when the brother who drove it drew out the nail at daybreak" (262-263). Buck and Buddy observed the letter of the custom that Negroes must be confined at night, but violated its spirit in order to grant the Negroes their inclination, their individuality, their liberty to do as they pleased.[6]

It is not clear in "The Bear" that Buck and Buddy had a conscious, formulated creed or program. Ike views their attempt to remedy the inhumanity of slavery as admirable but tentative. But they did at least recognize that a man is a man without regard to color and that he has a right to his own dignity. They dealt with their Negroes gently and without coercion. They apparently maintained their plantation on something approaching

---

[5] The effeminacy is certain and the homosexuality is probable in the light of the episode of Brownlee's later reappearance (292-293). The homosexuality is made virtually certain by the obscure joke Faulkner gives to Uncle Buddy, the suggestion that Brownlee, still hanging about the plantation, be renamed "Spintrius" (265). The allusion is to the *spintriae,* the practitioners of perversion described in Suetonius, *Tiberius* 43, and mentioned in *Caligula* 16 and *Vitellius* 3.

[6] On the custom of confining slaves at night, see John Spencer Bassett, *The Plantation Overseer,* in *A Southern Reader,* ed. Willard Thorp (New York, 1955), p. 181.

a cooperative or communal basis. They accepted, in short, that man is an end, not a means, and Ike gratefully receives their example in the hope of bettering it in his own life.[7]

The story of the fourth legacy, that left by Ike's Uncle Hubert Beauchamp, is told in another digression in Part IV of "The Bear" (300-308). The legacy is a gift made to Ike as a baby, which he is to open at twenty-one. It is sealed in burlap in the presence of the adult McCaslins—a silver cup containing fifty pieces of gold. The parcel is brought out on exhibit from time to time during Ike's childhood. It early changes weight and shape and ring, but Ike declines to open it until he is twenty-one, even when urged at the deathbed of his Uncle Hubert. When he does open it on his twenty-first birthday, he finds not what had originally been wrapped in the burlap but a shiny tin coffee-pot containing a few copper coins and a nest of I.O.U.'s from his uncle. Ike accepts the shrunken legacy with pleasure, "standing quietly beside the table and looking peacefully at the coffee-pot." Its material worthlessness gratifies him by confirming and by not disturbing his resolve, which accompanies his rejection of the plantation, to live henceforth on no greater means than will keep him very simply. Further, its worthlessness symbolizes his amused approval of his improvident Uncle Hubert.

When Ike's father and mother married, around 1860, they moved into the McCaslin mansion and finished it, at his mother's insistence. Sophonsiba Beauchamp had lived for years with her brother in the moldering ruin of a great house, a house which had four chimneys and contained "fine furnishings, the rosewood and mahogany and walnut." She aspired romantically to the grand style, posting a boy with a fox-horn at the gate of the Beauchamp place to summon passers-by to meals, and fancifully tracing the Beauchamp ancestry to the medieval Earls of Warwick. When she married Buck, she left Hubert behind in the old house, no doubt to the relief of "that bluff burly roaring childlike man." It was he who had let the Beauchamp place run down, and after his sister left, as Uncle Buddy put it, "Beauchamp fiddled while Nero [a dog] fox-hunted." Ike remembers the occasion when as a child he visited Hubert with his mother and they found an octoroon girl installed in the house. His mother ejected the intruder in a frenzy of outraged respectability, and his uncle, bowing to the whirlwind, seemed merely baffled by her interference in his way of life. He devoted himself,

---

[7] The code by which Buck and Buddy live is exhibited more fully and exactly in the story "Was" in Go Down, Moses. A creed and a program are attributed to them in an account written several years earlier than "The Bear" and inconsistent with it in a few small matters; it is found in "Retreat," The Unvanquished, pp. 52-61.

evidently, to pleasure—to a lazy and irresponsible life of hunting, eating, and wenching—and Ike's gold and silver went by driblets to support it. At length, after most of the Beauchamp horses and Negroes were gone, the old house inexplicably caught fire one night and burned to the ground. Hubert came to live with the McCaslins for the brief remainder of his life.

Hubert did not so much stand opposed to Sophonsiba's aggressive gentility and her romanticizing the plantation into a medieval fief, as he simply failed to comprehend them. He did not deliberately reject the hopes, the grand design expressed in the Beauchamp establishment, but was invulnerable to them. He existed throughout his life in a state of " inviolable and immortal adolescence," both his own improvidence and others' assaults upon it a perpetual puzzle to him. But Ike approves his choice; though innocently and unreflectively made, it was a good one. Hubert cared little for possessions—land, house, horses, slaves. He thought money was to be spent at need. He exploited no man. His very irresponsibility, contrasted for example with Carothers' way of life, had a positive moral quality. The coffee-pot and the coppers stand for Ike as symbols of a life shiftless and hedonistic but not wasted, a life acceptable for the evils it avoided.

Ike's explanation of why he refuses to accept his grandfather's plantation occupies the bulk of Part IV of "The Bear." He makes his explanation to McCaslin Edmonds, his cousin and guardian, in the commissary on an October afternoon and evening in 1888—presumably his twenty-first birthday. What Ike says takes the form of an elaborate history of the world, the United States, and the South, converted into an Old Testament narrative. In Eden, according to Ike's version, man was "to hold the earth mutual and intact in the communal anonymity of brotherhood," but in his presumption man lost Eden. The history of the Western world down to the Renaissance—"the five hundred years of absentee landlords in the Roman bagnios, and the thousand years of wild men from the northern woods who dispossessed them and devoured their ravished substance"—was the history of endless conflict over land and exploitation of it by its possessors. Then the discovery of America, a virgin continent, offered men the opportunity to re-establish the moral condition of Eden. But the New World was cursed from the beginning by the importation of slavery and (though Ike does not explicitly say so) of the institution of ownership of land. Slavery was an abomination in the sight of God, and though many men opposed it by the middle of the nineteenth century, few understood the nature of the abomination. It was an academic abstraction to abolitionists, a means of earning votes or speaker's fees to demagogues, a source of profit to manufacturers

or shippers involved in the cotton economy. John Brown alone saw it for
what it was—"among that loud and moiling all of them just one simple
enough to believe that horror and outrage were first and last simply horror
and outrage." Like Noah, Brown found grace in the eyes of the Lord, and
like the Biblical flood, the Civil War overwhelmed the South. The War,
Ike tells his incredulous cousin, was a benevolent visitation, God's attempt
to purge the South of the abomination. Afterward, during Reconstruction,
"three separate peoples had tried to adjust . . . to one another"—the black
sons of Ham, the defeated Southern whites, and the exploiters of human
misery and helplessness and ignorance who descended upon the South. But,
as Ike sees in 1888, the abomination has not been destroyed and will not
be destroyed for many years; the Negroes remain in bondage to the plantation and its fields.

The Biblical parallels in Ike's narrative are shifting and inexact, but
they illuminate his central proposition: that ownership of men and land
blight civilization and render it accursed. His concern is less with the history
of the South than with an inner individual orientation toward men and
land which the South institutionalized, the orientation represented in gross
form by his grandfather. He seems to accept, just as he accepts hunting,
that the impulse to use and hence to violate is innate in men, or at least is
an eternal temptation to men. But he posits the condition of Eden as an
ideal for human striving—not a state of innocence, but a condition in which
nature and men are ends in themselves. The patterns of such a condition he
has found in Sam Fathers, who achieved a close relation with nature, and
his father and Uncle Buddy, who strove to establish a just relation with men.
Though he cannot bring about single-handed "the communal anonymity of
brotherhood," he can accept the burden of past failures to perceive and
revere the ideal, and atone for them in his own life by dissociating himself
from the use of land or men as means.

One may question whether Ike's virtue is active, whether his rejection
of the legacy engages him in forwarding the ideal and defeating the evil
he has discovered.[8] On the day after his explanation to McCaslin Edmonds,
he moves from the plantation to a rented room in town. He buys carpenter's
tools and goes to work with his hands. In a sense, he can do no more, for
the evil he perceives is not something to be eradicated by supporting a

---

[8] Faulkner himself has raised doubts in subsequent comments on "The Bear." See
Cynthia Grenier, "The Art of Fiction: An Interview with William Faulkner,"
Accent, XVI (1956), 175, and *Faulkner in the University*, ed. Gwynn and Blotner
(Charlottesville, Va., 1959), pp. 245-246.

cause, joining a movement, or preaching a gospel; it is an individual matter of "the heart's truth" being obscured by "the heart's driving complexity," a failure not subject to correction by organizations or rational persuasion. Also, he too is human, and he must guard his ideal from himself. Some time after leaving the plantation he marries the daughter of his partner in carpentering. She learns of the legacy that is his if he will only claim it, though she evidently knows nothing of the reasons why he has not claimed it. She speaks of it as "our farm" and insistently asks when they are to move to it. Finally she attempts literally to seduce him into acquiescence. He resists up to the moment of sexual contact and then agrees, thinking, not only of his wife but of his own susceptibility, "*She is lost. She was born lost. We were all born lost.*" The lapse is fleeting, but it brings Ike, in the very moment it occurs, to a realization that the temptation is his as it is every man's and that he must be vigilant against it.

But it must be said that when Ike can act toward another person in accord with his ideal, he does so unstintingly. There are descendants from Carothers McCaslin's act of incest—the children of Tomey's Terrel, who is both the old man's son and his grandson, and Tennie Beauchamp, once a slave belonging to Hubert Beauchamp. In 1885, on his twenty-first birthday, Tennie's Jim, the eldest surviving child, flees north from the plantation in an unexplained gesture of repudiation. Ike, at nineteen, traces him into Tennessee—not to bring him back or coerce him in any other way but to deliver the legacy of $1000 which Uncle Buck and Uncle Buddy have established for each of the children of Tomey's Terrel. Ike fails to find him after two weeks' search and has to return the money to his cousin. In the following year, the next oldest child, Fonsiba, marries at seventeen a Negro from the North and goes away to live. As soon as a letter comes locating her in Arkansas, Ike goes to deliver her $1000, accepting the journey as an urgent personal responsibility. He finds her in a clumsily-built log cabin situated in a "waste of unfenced fallow and wilderness jungle," and her husband

> sitting there in the only chair in the house, before that miserable fire for which there was not wood sufficient to last twenty-four hours, in . . . a pair of gold-framed spectacles which, when he looked up and then rose to his feet, the boy saw did not even contain lenses, reading a book in the midst of that desolation, that muddy waste, fenceless and even pathless and without even a walled shed for stock to stand beneath: and over all, permeant, clinging to the man's very clothing and exuding from his skin itself that rank stink of baseless and imbecile delusion, that boundless rapacity and folly, of the carpet-bagger followers of victorious armies. (278)

Ike expostulates with him, but the man is undisturbed by the state of the "farm," a grant of his father for military service, and puts his reliance on the pension check that arrives on the first of every month. Ike bursts out with his view of the curse that has not yet been lifted from the South, but Fonsiba's husband affirms that the curse was voided by Lincoln's proclamation. Fonsiba, who is already a total stranger to Ike, seems to agree. In order to protect her, Ike banks her $1000 in the nearby town and arranges that three dollars will be delivered to her on the fifteenth of each month for the next twenty-eight years. In accepting responsibility to his Negro cousins, Ike implements his moral discovery as actively as, in its nature, it can be implemented.

3

The terms that I have repeatedly used to express the content of Ike's discovery are borrowed from Kant, for the second statement of the Categorical Imperative, if a slight addition is made, conveys as a maxim precisely the lesson Ike draws from his experience: "So act as to treat humanity, whether in thine own person or in that of any other, [and likewise to treat nature] in every case as an end withal, never as a means." The terms of the statement also apply at large to Faulkner's moral vision. It is not that Kant's maxim formulates a "lesson" to be derived from Faulkner's work, for the work is not didactic. Ike McCaslin is no mouthpiece for a sermon, but a human being working out his own destiny in the terms his experience furnishes. So are all of Faulkner's characters. But the opposition between men and nature as ends and men and nature as means dominates Faulkner's imagination and finds expression in the polarities that shape all his major works. Faulkner's consistent concern lies with human frustration and fulfillment. The polarities in his works—the balancing and opposing of character, the changes rung on situation and theme—invite his reader to find human frustration or failure where men and nature are exploited as means and to find human fulfillment where they become ends in themselves.

Faulkner's fiction enforces everywhere an intense and painful awareness of the difference between being a full and complete person and being an instrument, a thing, a symbol. It endlessly portrays both grossly and subtly insidious forms of enslavement and self-enslavement—economic exploitation, emotional or sexual exploitation, racism, subjection to machines, obsession with living up to the past, and life by formula (such as middle-class respectability or a puritanical sense of sin). It thus exhibits characters who become the instruments of something outside themselves that robs them of freedom and integrity. It also portrays the possibilities of fulfillment, of realizing what Faulkner called in the Nobel Prize speech "the old verities and truths of the heart"—"love and honor and pity and pride and compassion and sacrifice." He might have added sportsmanship and humility and loyalty and work and, above all, direct, warm personal relationships.[9]

This account of Faulkner's moral vision is related to three other accounts of it that have been proposed and widely considered by critics—that it represents a Christian view of man, that it represents "primitivism," and that it represents a rejection of "modernism." None of these three accounts is grossly or perversely mistaken, but each is in some degree off center. The account I propose differs from each of them but does not reject them wholly; what is at stake is a shifting of emphasis to avoid forcing Faulkner's work. A brief look at each of these accounts will clarify my own.

Up to a point, Faulkner's moral vision is in agreement with the Christian view of man. The Christian ethic is obviously very much involved in the opposition between men as means and as ends; Christ's teaching was of course that men should be treated as ends. Kant's second formulation of the Categorical Imperative is, in fact, a sophisticated restatement of the Golden Rule; Ike McCaslin thus discovers, in the terms his experience furnishes, the truth of the central Christian moral principle. Also, it is not in "The Bear" alone that there are suggestions of a universal human imperfection such as that accounted for in the myth of man's fall and the loss of paradise. Further, Faulkner's works often suggest that the meek shall indeed inherit the earth. But the fact remains that Faulkner does not convey a Christian version of man as do Greene and Eliot and Donne and even Pope. There is no concern with grace or revelation, with salvation or an Incarnation, no concern with supernaturalism at all. These things appear metaphorically or as aspects of characters' lives—those of Dilsey and Granny Millard, for example—but they do not shape the moral vision. Most important, there is in Faulkner's work no pervasive sense of sin—of human imperfection certainly, but not of universal human guilt. To equate Faulkner's moral vision to Christianity, thus, is to do less than justice to both.[1]

"Primitivism" denotes the idea that nature is a norm for judgment. In its most familiar form, the Rousseauist or romantic, it signifies that good is to be found in the natural, the simple, the unspoiled, the uncivilized, and

---

[9] The finest study yet made of Faulkner's moral vision, one with which my interpretation is largely in agreement, is that given in the revised version of Robert Penn Warren's classic essay on Faulkner, in *Selected Essays* (New York, 1958), pp. 59-79.
[1] The best case for Faulkner's moral vision being Christian is found in Waggoner, *William Faulkner*.

that civilization implies decline from the good and corruption of it. The case has been made for Faulkner's revering the life of nature and of his therefore finding human fulfillment in primitive and unsophisticated characters—children, Negroes, Indians, idiots, poor whites.[2] But this oversimplifies matters. There are, indeed, many characters in Faulkner's works who live close to nature or the soil, at peace with themselves and others, and who thereby fulfill themselves in some measure as human beings. But they are by no means all primitive and unsophisticated, as, for example, Sam Fathers is not. Further, there is no rigid scheme, no consistency to suggest that fulfillment is a consequence of being a poor white, an Indian, or a child. One cannot equate the Gowries of *Intruder in the Dust* with the McCallums of *Sartoris*, nor Doom of "A Justice" with Sam Fathers, nor Judith Sutpen as a child with Chick Mallison of the later novels. By a savage irony, Benjy Compson and Ike Snopes, the "idiots," achieve greater humanity than their "saner" opposite numbers, Jason Compson and Flem Snopes, but there is no suggestion that they represent an ideal of human fulfillment; the contrasts function in the works in which they appear, but not generally. Thus, though Faulkner seems to accept the simple and natural as conducive to fulfillment, he is not at all a primitivist valuing them for their own sake.

The third account of Faulkner's moral vision, the notion that it is a rejection of "modernism," contains a measure of truth, but it is sometimes too rigidly applied to the fiction and it attributes to Faulkner an interpretation of history that he may not hold. In so far as modernism implies exploiting nature and establishing human relationships that are mediated through power and ideology, it appears as an obstacle to human fulfillment. But this account tends to allegorize Faulkner's works inflexibly as a conflict between traditionalism and modernism, to find "good" characters affirming a traditional and humane ethic in their dealings with others and to find "bad" characters asserting freedom from such moral restraints.[3] Values in Faulkner's works are too fluid, too dependent upon context to submit to interpretation as consistent allegory. It is clearly impossible to classify all or even most of Faulkner's characters as belonging either to the "Sartoris world" or the "Snopes world." Furthermore, one questions whether the terms "modernism" and "traditionalism" are meaningfully applicable to Faulkner. The former is sometimes conceived as a condition in which firm

---

[2] Harry Modean Campbell and Ruel E. Foster, *William Faulkner: A Critical Appraisal* (Norman, Okla., 1951), pp. 148-158.

[3] See the well-known essays by George Marion O'Donnell and Malcolm Cowley in *Three Decades of Criticism*, pp. 82-109.

values are lacking, in which pragmatic standards rule and men feel lost
and aimless; it is sometimes identified with the influence of industrialism,
finance capitalism, and the power state. The latter, in contrast, is conceived
as a condition in which values are established and observed, in which men
know their identities as individuals and respect others' individuality; it
is sometimes identified with the influence of Christianity or aristocracy.[4] But
these are conditions that know no particular historical time; both pragmatism
and unselfish self-assurance are as old as humanity. To attribute a faith in
traditionalism to Faulkner is to foist upon him a special message about our
time that his works do not proclaim.

The polarity between men and nature as ends and as means is expressed
in Faulkner's work in many ways. It underlies the Faulknerian tragedy of
fulfillment missed or balked, of frustration grimly or gruesomely compen-
sated for—tragedy of a distinctive sort that does not usually resemble classical
tragedy. It underlies the comedy of "Was," the masterpiece among Faulkner's comic short stories, of *The Unvanquished*, and of the Snopes trilogy;
the comedy arises from characters' attempts to use or outsmart one another,
from their dogged resistance to being used, from their cleverness in sometimes foiling one another, and from their uncertainties over whether they
are using another or being used by him. It helps greatly to account for the
distinctive psychology of Faulkner's violent and driven characters, driven
almost invariably by being frustrated, victimized, or exploited. It helps also
to elucidate substantially, not only formally, the thematic organization of
Faulkner's novels, the structure of symbolic cross-reference that unites episodes or repeated versions of a story that often make up his novels. It is
impossible here to show at length how the moral vision is expressed, but its
expression can be exemplified by an examination of four broad types of
character that reappear frequently throughout Faulkner's works—the victim,
the self-enslaved, the exploiter, and the self-contained.

Faulkner's victims may be at the mercy of nature or circumstance, their
moral strength challenged and measured by their resistance. The tall convict
of "Old Man," for example, is buffeted about the lower Mississippi by a
raging flood until, with a kind of single-minded, unimaginative integrity,
he can successfully make his way back to the prison farm where he has
already been listed as drowned. Rider, the giant Negro laborer of "Pantaloon
in Black," loses his wife of only six months and expresses his prodigious
grief by handling alone a huge log at the sawmill where he works, by drink-

---

4 Warren, "Faulkner," *Selected Essays*, pp. 55-66.

ing a gallon of corn whiskey, and finally by killing a white man who uses loaded dice in a crap game. He is lynched, and the power of his feelings is ironically underlined afterward by the deputy sheriff who tells his bored wife that "niggers . . . ain't human," that they lack "the normal human feelings and sentiments of human beings." Mink Snopes, of *The Hamlet* and *The Mansion*, feels that he is the victim, as a poor sharecropper, of entrepreneurs and wealthier neighbors. When he is tried for the murder of a neighbor, his more successful cousin, Flem, offers him no assistance, and he waits out forty years on a prison farm to return and kill Flem. Each of these victims rises above the circumstances that threaten indifferently to break him, fights back at the world so that he is in some degree triumphant in defeat.

More often Faulkner's victims are at the mercy not of circumstances but of other people, and sometimes their fates are more harrowing and their ways of fighting back are more bizarre. Such a character is Miss Emily Grierson of "A Rose for Emily," who is a victim of her father's pride and her lover's callous indifference, and who compensates by killing her lover and sleeping for years beside the moldering corpse. The Negro slave in "Red Leaves" runs for six days through the wilderness, knowing he will finally be captured, to protest being made the victim of the Indian ritual in which a dead chief's horse and dog and servant are buried with him. In "Barn Burning," young Colonel Sartoris Snopes struggles against becoming a party to his barn-burning father's bitter vengefulness and in the end, with nowhere to go, can only flee in desperation. Each of these characters resists futilely others' attempts to make them instruments of a will not their own.

The victims whose situations are most fully explored by Faulkner are Caddy Compson and Joe Christmas, each of them ringed around and entrapped by people who would exploit them or who see in them only some abstract and symbolic value. Caddy, like all the members of her family, is first victimized by her whining, hypochondriac mother; all her children, possibly excepting her son Jason, are to Mrs. Compson no more than obstacles to her comfort and peace of mind. To her brother Quentin, Caddy is a vessel of morality, upholding honor or letting it fall as she is continent or incontinent. To Jason, she is a source of shame and, when he devises a scheme to blackmail and defraud her, of money. Her relationship with Benjy, though he loves her devotedly, is bound to be unsatisfactory to her; she is cast off by her husband; she is deprived of her baby as soon as it is born and thus deprived of expressing her love. In a sense Caddy is driven to

promiscuity in desperate search of warmth and intimate human contact. Her
natural vitality and emotional warmth demand expression, and all normal
expressions within her family are denied her. Her daughter, young Quentin,
though she lacks Caddy's vitality, is victimized with the same ferocity by some
of the same people and comes to a similar end. Faulkner himself most appro-
priately called *The Sound and the Fury* "the tragedy of two lost women."[5]

Joe Christmas is, as Alfred Kazin justly says, "an abstraction seeking
to become a human being."[6] His early life consists of repeated encounters
in which he dares others to treat him as a human being. Suspected of having
Negro blood, he is dealt with consistently as a symbol. Doc Hynes, his
grandfather and a believer in hellfire and brimstone; the children at the
orphanage; the dietician whose lovemaking he overhears; Bobby Allen,
the prostitute he falls in love with; Simon MacEachern, his rigidly Calvinist
foster father—all these reject and persecute him as being guilty of some
crime or sin whose nature he fails to comprehend. Then, as the crowning
indignity, Joanna Burden enters into sexual relations with him as an expression of her own confused guilt and compassion toward the Negro race.
Christmas is surrounded by people obsessed with sin and with the Negro;
he is to all of them the symbolic embodiment of the abstraction that obsesses
them. They deny him life and manhood. Neither Christmas nor Caddy can
maintain humanity when compelled by others to become the instrument of
their comfort or profit or the living symbol of a sin. Both are reduced to
things.

The second type of recurring character in Faulkner's work is the self-
enslaved person. Such people seek to live rigidly, by some abstract or ideal
principle, violating their own humanity and often that of others by forcing
it into a mold. Some are devoted to an uncompromising faith, like Doc
Hynes, MacEachern, and Joanna Burden. Others are aggressively conventional, like Sophonsiba Beauchamp, Mrs. Compson, and Cora Tull of *As
I Lay Dying*. Still others are idealists, devoted to an unworldly perfection
and confused by their failure to realize it. Such are the younger Bayard
Sartoris of *Sartoris*, Gail Hightower of *Light in August*, Quentin Compson
of *The Sound and the Fury*, and Thomas Sutpen of *Absalom, Absalom!*

Both Bayard and Hightower are bemused by their highly colored visions
of the military valor and glory of the past. Bayard, who survives a mecha-
nized war in which his twin brother has recklessly gotten himself killed, is

---

[5] Grenier, "The Art of Fiction," p. 173.
[6] "The Stillness of *Light in August*," *Three Decades of Criticism*, p. 252.

obsessed by the past glories of his own family. Some value that gleams in his great-grandfather's life as a Civil War colonel is missing from his world, a value his confusion never allows him to define but a value he fears his brother may have realized. He seeks it in speed and liquor and high jinks, but succeeds only in alarming his family, in precipitating his grandfather's fatal heart attack, and finally in producing his own futile death by a piece of daredeviltry. A similar obsession betrays Hightower not into frenetic action but into immobility and withdrawal. His grandfather had been killed in Jefferson during a Civil War raid; Hightower cannot forgive himself for not having died then and there and in that way. He marries the daughter of one of his seminary professors in order to arrange to be sent as minister to a Jefferson church. Then, after his self-absorption has driven his wife to drink, adultery, and perhaps suicide, and after his ravings about the Civil War from the pulpit have got him turned out of his church, he settles down to an obscure existence in Jefferson and lives in his private imagination of the War. He emerges from it just too late to save Joe Christmas from death.

Quentin Compson's hatred and fear of time is an index of his self-enslavement. He is bothered by the age-old problem of mutability and the modern, Dostoievskian problem of whether any stable values exist. He seeks an abstract, ideal concept of right and wrong, honor and dishonor, one that is proof against the ravages of time and change. Hence he sets an absolute value on Caddy's virginity and, once she has lost it, wishes to create a private hell by committing incest with her in order to prove to himself at least that an absolute evil exists. He, like Caddy, feels the lack of any moral and emotional center in the Compson family. Because his desire for moral certainty cannot be satisfied by the world of time and change, he commits suicide.

The demands Thomas Sutpen makes on the world are, to him in his invincible innocence, only reasonable demands. Having been turned away from the front door of a great house as a child, a child of simple mountaineers, he resolves to found a plantation, a house, a dynasty himself, and he asks only the opportunity to do so single-handed. He is absorbed by the dream, so much so that all who are close to him become only instruments or obstacles to its realization. He sets aside his first wife and son on learning that they are tainted with Negro blood, a violation of the conditions of gentility in the South. He reduces his second wife, Ellen Coldfield, to a fluttering, ineffectual, distracted person with his single-minded ambition. He tries to use his children to forward the dynasty and is balked when the son of his first marriage appears and becomes engaged to his daughter; he declines to get rid of the son by the simple means of acknowledging him as his son. Then he bitterly offends Rosa Coldfield by offering to marry her if she will first bear him a male child. And he is at last killed by Wash Jones, whose granddaughter he declines to marry, though she has borne him a child. His dream produces a shambles. Sutpen victimizes all those around him and they recoil upon him in hatred and resentment, thwarting his plan. Like the other self-enslaved characters, he is doomed to failure in his attempt to force the world into a mold.

The third type of character is that of the exploiter, the man who treats others knowingly and either sadistically or indifferently as objects or instruments. Military men often belong to this type. Percy Grimm of *Light in August* and Captain McLendon of "Dry September" both kill Negroes suspected of sleeping with white women. The old commander of *A Fable*, though a very different sort of man, justifies the continuance of the war and the execution of the corporal. The classic exploiters, however, are Popeye of *Sanctuary*, Jason Compson of *The Sound and the Fury*, and Flem Snopes of *The Hamlet, The Town* and *The Mansion*. They too are self-enslaved, knowingly and consciously enslaved by a vicious inhumanity. All three of them solitary and self-centered men, they do violence upon others without compunction.

Popeye's violence is literal physical violence. He kills Tommy and abandons Lee and Ruby Goodwin to the consequences. Impotent himself, he rapes Temple Drake with a corncob and later looks on while she has sexual relations with Red; unable to enjoy, he violates. When Temple takes refuge in Red's liking for her, Popeye has him killed, toying with Temple's desperate urge to escape and daring her to make the move that will result in Red's death. He is a city man, frightened by nature when not indifferent to it. In a sense he is a victim, cut off from life and joy by crippling inherited syphilis; his casual violence expresses in part despair, and in the end he hopelessly acquiesces in his conviction for a violent crime that he did not commit.

Jason's violence issues from a total lack of respect for anyone's emotions but his own. Thinking himself victimized by his family—not sent to Harvard as Quentin is, cheated of a job in a bank when Caddy's husband casts her off—he expresses his paranoia in calculating the advantages and liabilities that others are to him. Committed as a businessman to the appearance of respectability, he thinks of Benjy as a damaging public spectacle, of Caddy and Young Quentin as sources of scandal that reflect on his good name. Dilsey, with all her strength, he considers a parasite, an obstacle in his path. He blackmails Caddy into remaining away from home, and with elaborate chicanery steals for himself the money she sends for young Quentin. He is not only acquisitive but vindictive and petty, brutally foiling Caddy's love for her daughter and mercilessly baiting the others of his family. Balked in the end by young Quentin's theft of the money he has stolen from her, he is driven close to madness at the failure of his calculations, the affront to his rationality.

Flem's violence issues from the quiet, detached manipulations of the pure economic exploiter. He moves into Frenchman's Bend, where on one day a small farmer will give his neighbor no quarter in a horse trade and on the next will help him to plow his field. Flem adopts the horse-trading code by which any deception is fair and under which one trades at one's own risk, but in applying it he regards only his own gain and never the consequences to others. He is without feelings, pleasures, desires—inhuman in the way he acts toward the world, as though it exists only to be taken advantage of. He exacts usurious interest because those to whom he lends lack the wit to know they are being victimized. He plays upon the community's need for cheap horseflesh and fascination with it to victimize Armstid and others in the "Spotted Horses" episode. He uses his idiot cousin, Ike Snopes, for economic advantage. He marries the pregnant Eula Varner because the price is right, and later having moved into town and into a bank, compels her to suicide as an instrument of his drive for respectability. He is the coldest, purest exploiter in all of Faulkner's fiction.

These three types of character—the victim, the self-enslaved, and the exploiter—overlap in some ways. The conscious exploiter is sometimes a victim himself, and he often forces the world into a mold of his conceiving. The self-enslaved person is sometimes a victim and almost always an unconscious exploiter. The victim, in contrast, defensive rather than aggressive, seldom exploits or tries to implement an ideal. But the fourth type, the self-contained person, stands in contrast to the other three. He is the person who cannot be victimized because he is more or less inviolable. He is not self-enslaved because his acceptance of the physical world and his nearness to it make a rigid code or an unworldly ideal unnecessary to him. He is not an exploiter because he accords others the same dignity he possesses himself.

Some self-contained characters assume the burden of others' exploitation and dissociate themselves from it, as do Ike McCaslin and the corporal of *A Fable*. Some take upon themselves a responsibility for other people, guiding and supporting, opposing inhumanity, as do Granny Millard in *The Unvanquished*, Aunt Jenny DuPre in *Sartoris*, and Miss Habersham in *Intruder in the Dust*. Some, like Lena Grove in *Light in August* and Eula

Varner in *The Hamlet*, embody so absolutely the natural process of genera-
tion that they are almost natural creatures themselves, inviolable by exploitation. Some younger characters, like Chick Mallison in *Intruder in the Dust*
and Bayard Sartoris in *The Unvanquished*, move toward integrity much as
Ike McCaslin does, sifting experience for themselves and affirming their own
choice, against outer influences, to see men as ends in themselves. The most
absolutely self-contained of Faulkner's characters are Sam Fathers, Lucas
Beauchamp of *Intruder in the Dust*, Dilsey of *The Sound and the Fury*, and
V. K. Ratliff of *The Hamlet*.

Lucas, like Joe Christmas but more successfully, challenges the world
to treat him not as a Negro but as a man. His almost comic dignity and
reserve, his forthrightness, and his resistance to contradiction all proclaim
his will to be taken at his own valuation. Discovering a white man's crime,
he intervenes privately to see that restitution is made to the injured party.
When he is jailed for murder and threatened with lynching, he stands on
his dignity and declines to explain to someone who will not credit the truth
from a Negro, even though to speak might save him. In the end he insists
on paying the legal expenses, refusing to accept favors from anyone. Lucas
affirms his own integrity, which is very real, by main force of will.

Dilsey is great in her emotional strength, her power of understanding
and acceptance. Even in the nightmare of the Compson household, she rejects no one—not the whining Mrs. Compson, nor the retarded Benjy, nor
the promiscuous young Quentin, nor the sadistic Jason. She fetches and
carries to comfort Mrs. Compson. She sees that Benjy is supervised. She
intervenes in quarrels between Jason and young Quentin. Reproved for taking Benjy to her Negro church, she rejoins, accepting Benjy as a person,
that "de good Lawd don't keer whether he smart or not." She sees no sense
in the rejection of Caddy as a fallen woman. When Jason cuts off her wages,
her devotion is such that she remains, always the moral and emotional center
of the Compson family.

Ratliff stands as the counterpoise to Flem Snopes in *The Hamlet*. A mer-
chant like Flem, he accepts the relatively humane code of Frenchman's Bend
whereby one man may best another in a transaction but not injure him. He
observes the spreading success of Flem's operations and the confusion of
the country folk over whether Flem actually violates the code to exploit them
or merely operates within it as the most successful trader the community has
yet encountered. What the country people cannot articulate for themselves
about Flem's machinations, he points out to them—shrewdly, ironically, humorously. And he sets out to defeat Flem if he can do so, to best him in a

trade. His defeat at Flem's hands is perhaps the sign that no man who considers the humanity of his methods can beat another who lacks such scruples. Ratliff stands out as the most delightfully knowledgeable and articulate opponent of exploitation in all of Faulkner's works.

This classification of Faulkner's characters, though neither fixed nor exhaustive, indicates clearly the moral topography of his work. Its contours are perpetually determined by the polarity between man and nature as ends and as means. The self-contained, in their selfless integrity, represent human fulfillment. Victims of circumstances or exploitation who resist being victimized assert their humanity in the face of all odds. The self-enslaved move tragically and often threateningly within the closed circles of their private systems. The exploiters fail themselves and humanity, isolated by their failure of sympathy and their unawareness of their own nature. Yet all but the most abandoned exploiters possess some dignity, some worthiness of respect or pity. It is as if Faulkner were showing us the pervasive peril of becoming a means, a thing; the moral vision of his work lends support to his often repeated affirmation that the highest of virtues is endurance. His work is a great and exhaustively sensitive exploration of a familiar moral distinction.

FAULKNER'S EXISTENTIALIST
AFFINITIES

RALPH A. CIANCIO

THE EXISTENTIALIST, curiously enough, is a philosopher without a philosophy. That is, Existentialism is more a philosophical attitude, a special *way
of thinking*, than a systematic body of thought. Although it has flowered
as an intellectual movement only recently, men in almost every age have
commented, as did Pascal, on the dreadful experience of being "engulfed
in the infinite immensity of spaces of which I am ignorant, and which know
me not." At the roots of the family tree of Existentialism in fact are Hera-
cleitus, Socrates, the Stoics, and St. Augustine; Kierkegaard is the bole.
From Nietzsche and Dostoevsky it acquired nourishment and impetus. It
should not be surprising, therefore, to find existential thinking being expressed today, consciously or unconsciously, by writers outside the main
stream of contemporary European thought.

The critics on occasion have pointed out William Faulkner's affinities
with both Christian and non-Christian Existentialists,[1] especially with the
latter in France, among whom he is influential and revered (the late Albert
Camus referred to him as *"le plus grand ecrivain contemporain"*); and

---

[1] Hyatt H. Waggoner, *William Faulkner: From Jefferson to the World* (Lexington,
Ky., 1959), pp. 84, 86, 109-112, 113-114, 119, 240, 251, 257, 271; Harry Modean
Campbell and Ruel E. Foster, *William Faulkner: A Critical Appraisal* (Norman, Okla.,
1951), p. 124; Robert M. Slabey, "Joe Christmas, Faulkner's Marginal Man," *Phylon*,
XXI (1960), 266-277, and "Myth and Ritual in *Light in August*," *Studies in Liter-
ature and Language*, II (1960), 328-349.

Tennessee Williams has spoken of a "common link"—"a sense, an intuition, of an underlying dreadfulness in modern experience"—between the Gothic school of American writers, of which Faulkner is the acknowledged master, and the philosophical school of Jean Paul Sartre.[2] But Faulkner's affinities with the Existentialists go much deeper than any of his commentators have thus far intimated: Yoknapatawpha County, it can be said, is existentially oriented.

I do not mean to suggest that Faulkner has purposely stuffed his novels with Existentialist ideology. Indeed, Faulkner may have no philosophical knowledge of Existentialism whatsoever, nor care to have.[3] He is simply and profoundly a great artist, not a philosopher. But that is just the point: a kinship exists between artistic expression and Existentialism, and often the Existentialist is more at home with the artist than with other philosophers. It is not mere coincidence that the Existentialists are preoccupied with art. Sartre writes novels, short stories, and dramas; Gabriel Marcel is a playwright and a music and literary critic; Karl Jaspers has made studies of tragic drama; Camus was a Nobel Prize novelist; and Martin Heidegger derives his inspiration from the poetry of Hölderlin and Rilke. In the following pages I hope to make evident that Faulkner's methodology—his style and technique—lends itself to an existential awareness of reality (Part 2) and, more extensively, that his world abounds with both negative and positive Existentialist themes (Parts 3 and 4).

2

We can better appreciate Faulkner's methodology if we understand the fraternal relationship between art and Existentialism. It derives from the ontological reunification of the world. Ever since Descartes dichotomized the world into two separate entities, mind and matter, the disciplines have been accustomed to regarding the world as that which is external to man. The ego, according to Descartes, is an incarcerated, self-enclosed substance. But contrary to Descartes the Existentialist maintains that the world transcends any objective-subjective dichotomy because it is the aggregate of both elements. What we call the objective world is only one dimension of the total world, which comprehends *my* world and *your* world as well as the

---

[2] Introduction to Carson McCullers, *Reflections in a Golden Eye* (New York, 1958), pp. x-xi.
[3] Faulkner is familiar with the novels of Sartre and Camus, but his knowledge of their philosophical positions—especially in regard to Camus—is dubious. See *Faulkner in the University*, ed. Frederick L. Gwynn and Joseph L. Blotner (Charlottesville, Va., 1959), p. 161.

objective world. From their respective standpoints science and philosophy can reflect on phenomena and experience commonly known to all men because they abstract from the world. But this is not the way each of us, as an individual, faces the world in daily life. The world we encounter every day consists of a conglomeration of myriad and complex facts; it does not manifest itself as a syllogism. It includes our personal past and, in a sense, our personal future; since life is a continuum no advent or action is without its inherent past and future. The world, in other words, is personal as well as public, subjective as well as objective, and hence neither because both. Man encounters the world in his openness to it, with his total self, in the concrete experience of, to use Heidegger's phrase, "being-in-the-world-to-gether-with-others." This is Heidegger's way of saying that man is not *in* the world, but rather *of* the world.[4]

The concrete experience of being-in-the-world-together-with-others is the Existentialist's primordial datum, his starting point. As one would suppose, the corollary to this radical, pre-Socratic orientation is a radical methodology. If the world comprehends personal as well as public existence, the Existentialist, in traditional terminology, is at once the object and subject of his thinking; *a priori* one with the world, he himself participates in his primordial datum. Therefore he can not—and this is the crux of Existentialism—philosophize from a particular standpoint outside the world, but rather must philosophize from within the world; not by standing aloof from the world, but by actively deepening his primordial experience of it; not by reflecting on it, but by boring into it with his total self.

This is a far cry from the traditional view which holds that the intellect alone is sacred and that the philosopher, in order to unfetter his intellect and to safeguard it against a distorted perspective, must detach himself from the life around him. To the Existentialist such an approach defeats itself. Like the halfback of anecdotal fame, the philosopher who detaches himself from the life around him puts on a dazzling performance but leaves the ball behind; he philosophizes in a vacuum. The Existentialist rather copes with the world as the world is given—to the total self. He knows that there are two ways in which we apprehend the world: by thinking about it and by living in it. But there is always something in thought that transcends thought, namely experience; and there is always something in experience that transcends experience, namely thought. He therefore philosophizes on

---

[4] Here I have followed John Wild's helpful critique, "Existentialism as a Philosophy," *The Journal of Philosophy*, LVII (1960), 45-62; also see William Barrett, *Irrational Man* (New York, 1958), pp. 193-194.

72   STUDIES IN FAULKNER

both the levels of thought and experience simultaneously: he philosophizes
with his entire being.

It is easy to see why Existentialism gives special credence to art. Since a
knowledge of the world as it is experienced from within is vital to a
knowledge of the world in general, the artist occupies a singularly congenial
position for presenting the world as a totality. Specifically, art and Existentialism are fraternal for basically four interrelated reasons: (1) Like Existentialism, any worthy aesthetic begins in concrete experience and not with
abstractions. Art proper is never reflective in a dialectical sense; the artist
knows that life can only be illumined by more life, not by boneless, fleshless
theories applied to life. Similarly, the Existentialist does not reflect on the
drama of life from an aloof sphere of preconceived notions about life.
(2) Neither art nor Existentialism restricts phenomena *a priori*. Each pre-
supposes nothing and supposes everything. Just as any experience is grist
for the artist's mill, nothing in experience is irrelevant to the Existentialist.
To be sure, the artist selects his means, he keeps his chock and chisel handy;
but before the artistic process is under way (and more often during it) the
artist freely draws on anything within human conception for his material.
(3) Existentialism accentuates and is deeply engrossed in concrete personal
experiences which hitherto have been considered philosophically only as
abstractions but without which art is not art at all—the non-rational phenomena of the human spirit: death, anxiety, freedom, and, as Faulkner
puts it, "love and honor and pity and pride and compassion and sacrifice."
Such phenomena contribute to the Existentialist's primordial datum, in
which his thinking is grounded. (4) Finally, the thought content of art
proper is always a concrete living experience expressed existentially. In the
introduction to his trilogy *The Drama of the Soul*, Marcel cites the following
passage from Gerhart Hauptmann as a description of the kind of thinking
peculiar to drama and, he suggests, to art in general: "We must distinguish
between thought in the process of being thought and thought which has
been expressed already. It is the first of these which must express itself,
thought at the very moment of birth before the umbilical cord is broken. It is
perhaps like the thought of a man born blind, when his eyes are opened to
the light for the first time."[5] Thought in art, that is to say, is experiential
thinking, or to borrow terms Marcel uses elsewhere, *thinking thought* as
distinguished from *thought thought*. As I have indicated above, experiential
thinking is invaluable to the Existentialist because it is total-self thinking.

---

[5] Preface to *Three Plays*, trans. Rosaline Wood (New York, 1958), p. 14.

Contrary to what some critics have maintained, however, Existentialism and artistic expression are not identical. Their affinity for each other may be synthesized—and here I risk an oversimplification—in one central idea: they both allow the world to reveal itself as a totality. They differ in that Existentialism proceeds to reflect on the self-revelation of the world, but without this primordial experience Existentialism—indeed, all philosophical thinking—is doomed to half-truths. In a certain sense it can be said that the experience art reveals is pre-Existentialism if it is remembered that such priority is strictly formal; Existentialism never departs from its initial experience of the self-revelation of the world.

The self-revelation of the world is precisely what we find in Faulkner, to whom we are now prepared to turn. In no other novelist is the existential way of thinking so closely paralleled aesthetically. His methodology—his style and technique—has one fundamental aim: to comprehend experience as a totality by encountering it from within.

So tightly intertwined are Faulkner's style and technique that it is difficult to write about one without including the other. But to begin, consider his use of the multiple point of view. One of the virtues of this technique is its comprehensiveness; it makes possible the illumination of experience from various angles and thereby increases the reader's—and the writer's—understanding of that experience. In regard to the genesis of *The Sound and the Fury*, for instance, Faulkner has said that he had told the story of Caddy once but sought to understand it by retelling it three more times: hence the four points of view in that novel.[6] This technique, of course, would be conducive to comprehensive awareness in any author. But Faulkner endows it with a peculiar repetitiveness which contributes even more. Just as Existentialism gains its insights by boring further into its subject rather than by abstracting from it, Faulkner deepens our understanding of a story not by pondering it from without, but by subjecting himself and the reader to the experience of the story, again and again. In *Absalom, Absalom!* the story of Sutpen's monomaniacal quest for social acceptance and of Bon's alienation, with most of its essential details, is told four times. Each time it is retold it is relived; it is further bored into and more is revealed. Yet no one retelling supersedes its predecessor, nor are any essentials dropped; just as the Existentialist never departs from his primordial experience, everything is carried along and seen in the light of the whole. In fact we do not understand the beginning of that novel until we have

6 *Faulkner in the University*, p. 1.

reached its end. Faulkner, to borrow a statement from Coleridge, "like the motion of a serpent, . . . at every step . . . pauses and half recedes, and from the retrogressive movement collects the force which again carries him onward." This same kind of repetitiveness, although to a lesser extent, occurs in *As I Lay Dying* and *The Sound and the Fury*.

Complementing in purpose his use of the multiple point of view is Faulkner's circumspection, his stylistic tendency to speculate and probe. He rarely settles for the first word his daemon gives him. He either refrains from making positive assertions by means of what Warren Beck calls "the statement of alternatives"[7]—"He was the first one, standing lounging trying to look occupied or at least innocent"—or postpones them until he has relentlessly probed, torn away at his subject through a process of negation:

> To them, Miss Rosa must not have been anything at all now: not the child who had been the object and victim of the vanished aunt's vindictive and unflagging care and attention, and not even the woman which her office as housekeeper would indicate, and certainly not the factual aunt herself. (*Absalom, Absalom!*, 70)
> . . . a little dog, nameless and mongrel and many fathered, grown yet weighing less than six pounds, who couldn't be dangerous because there was nothing anywhere much smaller, not fierce because that would have been called just noise, not humble because it was already too near the ground to genuflect, and not proud because. . . . (*Go Down, Moses*, 296)

This process is Faulkner's stratagem for cutting through adventitious crust to lay bare the truth. In this sense Faulkner, like all Existentialists, is a phenomenologist—he attempts to go to *die Sachen selbst*. He keeps to primordial experience by bracketing or holding off observations rendered from a mediating standpoint outside the experience. I do not mean to suggest, of course, that once we "get through" Faulkner's probings and stratagems—in sum, his methodology—we shall have arrived at the story. In the same sense that the Existentialist's prolonged engagement with his primordial experience constitutes his philosophy, Faulkner's methodology *is* the story.

Again, the lengthy, circumambient sentences which characterize Faulkner's style are also suited to a comprehensive purpose. To a group of students at the University of Virginia, Faulkner stated: ". . . to me, no man is himself, he is the sum of his past. There is no such thing really as was because the past is. It is a part of every man, every woman, and every moment. All of his and her ancestry, background, is all a part of himself and herself at

---

7 "William Faulkner's Style," *William Faulkner: Three Decades of Criticism*, ed. Frederick J. Hoffman and Olga W. Vickery (East Lansing, Mich., 1960), p. 151.

any moment. And so a man, a character in a story at any moment of action is not just himself as he is then, he is all that made him. . . ."[8] The idea expressed here, as I have suggested above, is based on the existential awareness of Time as a "living" quality. Time is integral; it includes not only the past but the future as well; *is* in reality encompasses *was* as well as *will be.* Faulkner consequently attempts "to get his [a character's] past and possibly his future into the instant in which he does something."[9] The lengthy sentence, in other words, is an attempt to crystalize experience as a totality, to render temporality spatially, and hence the circumambience; Janus-faced, his sentences look forward and backward simultaneously. This aim also accounts for his style's repetitiveness, and also for the frequent parentheses:

> So he sent word in by one of the others (he was not married then either) that he would not be home, and he and Sutpen went on until the light failed. Two of the niggers (they were thirteen miles from Sutpen's camp then) had already gone back to get blankets and more grub. . . . That was how Grandfather remembered it: he and Sutpen leading their horses (he would look back now and then and see the horses' eyes shining in the torch light and the horses' tossing and the shadows slipping along their shoulders and the flanks) and the dogs and the niggers (niggers mostly still naked except for a pair of pants here and there). . . . (*Absalom, Absalom!*, 245)

As someone has cogently said, Faulkner envelops rather than develops a story.

But Faulkner, like the Existentialist, places little faith in a comprehensive view which fails to emanate from within. Pride, compassion, and sacrifice are affairs of the heart, not of the intellect; we understand such experiences only through participation, not by examining them as objects, as things which stand against us and oppose us. Subjectivity in fact is the generating power in Faulkner's world; it makes it palpitate. His characters—excluding certain characters in his later novels, especially the spectator-philosopher Gavin Stevens—are in some way personally involved in the action they relate, so that their observations are fraught with passion. Even Shreve, who in *Absalom, Absalom!* is detached from Southern tradition and therefore not immediately involved in its degeneracy, has his own special bias. Faulkner purposely "engages" his characters because their subjective, total-self response to experience lends it a validity otherwise unattainable. This is even true when he depicts his characters by means of stream of consciousness, one of Faulkner's favorite techniques, adopted to make accessible primordial in-

---

8 *Faulkner in the University*, p. 84; also see p. 139.
9 *Faulkner in the University*, p. 84.

ternal man. Ordinarily stream-of-consciousness writers depict the psychic movement of their characters detached from the dramatic context of the story. But in Faulkner, as Robert Humphrey illustrates, stream of consciousness and external action are synthesized in a plot.[1]

Or, to put it another way, Faulkner's mode of thought is clearly experiential. It is being lived the very moment it is being thought. His characters do not reflect objectively on the experience of the moment; they live it. They are not mouthpieces for Faulkner; Faulkner is their mouthpiece. This is why *The Hamlet* seems to me superior to *The Town*: what is expressed in *The Hamlet* is born of the experience contained in that very novel, whereas what is expressed in *The Town* is a reflection on what occurs in *The Hamlet*. Thought and experience in the later novel are not coeval, are not co-originated.

Of its nature experiential thinking will not always express itself according to semantic proprieties. Hence the logic of Faulkner's statements, his metaphors, and his oxymorons often "leave his reader with suspensions which are not resolvable in rational terms," as Walter J. Slatoff has so acutely demonstrated.[2] But in view of Faulkner's aim, this is to be expected. Someone once wisely remarked that lucidity is a semantic virtue, but not necessarily an aesthetic or philosophical one. The point is that the experience Faulkner subjects us to transcends logic. His interest is the world as it reveals itself—"the moil and seethe of humanity," as he refers to it—which is neither logical nor illogical but rather a-logical; all-inclusive, it inevitably yokes together non-rational disparates which can not be analyzed. Slatoff is correct, it seems to me, in suggesting that Faulkner actually allows suspensions to assert themselves, for suspensions are common to our experience in the actual world. To sum up, what Slatoff writes about Faulkner's use of the oxymoron applies to his methodology in general: "Its validity is usually intuitive and emotional rather than logical or intellectual. It does not so much explore or analyze a condition as render it forcefully."[3]

3

Given Faulkner's methodology, it is not surprising that his fictional world abounds with Existentialist themes. They can be illumined best by

---

[1] *Stream of Consciousness in the Modern Novel* (Berkeley, 1954), pp. 105-111.
[2] "The Edge of Order: the Pattern of Faulkner's Rhetoric," *Three Decades of Criticism*, p. 178.
[3] *Three Decades of Criticism*, p. 177

juxtaposing the Existentialist world with Yoknapatawpha County. The following are a few basic Existentialist ideas as set forth by Sartre, Camus, and Heidegger.[4]

By virtue of his consciousness, man, says Sartre, is different from other beings in the world. Objects or anything which is simply and fully "there," in Sartre's terminology, is "Being-in-itself" (*L'Être-en-soi*) as distinguished from "Being-for-itself" (*L'Être-pour-soi*), which is man. Being-in-itself is complete, dense, substantial; Being-for-itself, on the other hand, is incomplete, gelatinous, vacuous. The first is positive because it is full Being, the latter is its own Nothingness. Sartre, standing traditional philosophy on its head, thinks of consciousness as a hole within us, as a vacuum—in his own words, as an "obscene superfluity." His position can be stated concisely in a perverted Cartesian proposition: "I think, therefore I am not." What Sartre wishes to emphasize is that man, as consciousness, as Being-for-itself, has no essence, no inherent meaning or definition. Man is a free-floating consciousness divorced from all ties, a project continuously moving into the future. Only through action, which becomes the In-itself of the For-itself when realized, does he appropriate meaning. Hence Sartre's famous dictum: existence precedes essence.

The world man projects himself into is nihilistic. To start with there is no Divine guidance. Sartre quotes Dostoievsky—"If God didn't exist, everything would be possible"—and says that "this is the very starting point of Existentialism."[5] Sartre posits several arguments for the non-existence of God, but here we need cite only his principal one. It is simply this. If Being-for-itself is always becoming, God, who is the perfection of Being-for-itself, is complete and therefore no longer becoming. That is, God is Absolute

---

4 Some will object to having Camus called an Existentialist thinker. This objection is based largely on the publicized Camus-Sartre feud over political ideology and Hegel's philosophy of history, and especially on Camus' belief in values pre-existent to action: "An analysis of rebellion leads us to the suspicion that, contrary to the postulates of contemporary thought, a human nature does exist, as the Greeks believed" (*The Rebel*, trans. Anthony Bower [New York, 1954], p. 22). In other words, Camus disagrees with Sartre's view that existence precedes essence. But these divergences do not preclude likeness of thought between the two men, nor do they constitute outright opposition. (See Jacques Ehrmann, "Camus and the Existentialist Adventure," and Henri Peyre, "Camus the Pagan," *Yale French Studies*, XXV [1960], 93-97, 20.) Sartre, moreover, is not the only Existentialist—not even *the* Existentialist, as is sometimes presumed—and one need not abide by his dicta to be of Existentialist persuasion; Jaspers, Heidegger, and Marcel in fact have sought to have their thinking disassociated from Sartre's. Camus himself said that, although he could not accept the conclusions of his compatriot, he favored other Existentialist thinkers: "If the premises of existentialism are to be found, as I believe they are, in Pascal, Nietzsche, Kierkegaard or Chestov, then I agree with them" (*Albert Camus: A Final Interview* [New York, 1960], p. 36).
5 *Existentialism*, trans. Bernard Frechtman (New York, 1947), p. 51.

Consciousness or *En-soi-pour-soi*, a self-contradictory concept; if God were
one with full Being, He would not be a conscious Being. Camus, who abided
by neither Sartre's premises nor his terms, would insist that man, to the
contrary, does have a nature and hence existence does not precede essence.
But because a transcendent Being is beyond the human condition, such a
Being can not be meaningful, let alone rationalized: "I don't know whether
this world has a meaning that transcends it. But I know that I do not know
that meaning, and that it is impossible for me just now to know it. What
can a meaning outside my condition mean to me? I can understand only in
human terms. What I touch, what resists me—that is what I understand."[6]
In Sartre's orientation the concept of God is illogical; in Camus's it is black-
balled. To Heidegger, whether God exists is irrelevant to his ontology and
the question has been postponed for later consideration. At the moment it
is clear, however, that he rejects the traditional concept of God.

The corollary to God's death is catastrophic. Sartre states it as follows:
"The existentialist . . . thinks it very distressing that God does not exist,
because all possibility of finding values in a heaven of ideas disappears along
with him; there can no longer be *a priori* Good, since there is no infinite
and perfect consciousness to think it. Nowhere is it written that the Good
exists, that we must be honest, that we must not lie; because the fact is we
are on a plane where there are only men."[7] Without God man is spiritually
homeless, a pet existential theme. Nothing is sacred *a priori*, there are no
signposts to guide his moral life. He is condemned to be free in a direction-
less world. According to Heidegger, modern man is too late for the Attic
deities, too soon for the God of the future. In Camus, spiritual homelessness
is reflected in the very titles of his stories: *The Stranger, The Fall, Exile and
the Kingdom.*

But even if God did exist, man would still have to cope with the indifferent universe. In his quest for meaning and the appropriation of the
In-itself, man longs to abjure his freedom and to become one with full
Being—that is, he longs to become a "thing." This, says Sartre, is the fundamental relation between consciousness and full Being. But Being-in-itself,
because dense and indifferent, withstands man; the universe is an impene-
trable wall. But the universe can be indifferent only in relation to itself; in
relation to man's aspirations, indifference becomes hostility. As a result,
consciousness and the universe are in opposition. Being-in-itself, moreover,

6 *The Myth of Sisyphus and Other Essays*, trans. Justin O'Brien (New York, 1955),
p. 51.
7 *Existentialism*, pp. 26-27.

encroaches upon man's freedom in that it limits it, rebuffs it, and forces it to face up to its own facticity, its own contingency. The awareness of one's contingency produces *la nausée*.

In the world of Camus this fundamental enmity between the universe and consciousness is one of the constituent walls of *l'absurde*. On a biological level man communes with the universe, but in his conscious relation to it man is a stranger, an exile. What teleological design man has hitherto discerned in the cosmos, according to Camus, is a man-made illusion:

> At the heart of all beauty lies something inhuman, and these hills, the softness of the sky, the outline of these trees at this very minute lose the illusory meaning with which we had clothed them, henceforth more remote than a lost paradise. The primitive hostility of the world rises up to face us across millennia. For a second we cease to understand it because for centuries we have understood in it solely the images and designs we had attributed to it beforehand, because henceforth we lack the power to make use of that artifice. The world evades us because it becomes itself again. The stage scenery masked by habit becomes again what it is . . . perhaps we shall come even to desire what suddenly leaves us alone. But that time has not yet come. Just one thing: that denseness and that strangeness of the world is the absurd.[8]

Life's absurdity is intensified since man, if he chooses to live authentically, sees that existence is "conditioned by death." The reality of man's inevitable annihilation is a presence he cannot elude, and toward which, according to Heidegger, he is "forward-running." Death is a presence—not something confronted in the future, not something which stands ahead of him like some remote beacon perceivable at a distance. Man is bounded by death; it is a part of the structure of his existence, as is the rind of an apple to its fruit. It is also the inexorable termination of man's drive to complete himself, the impossibility of possibilities. Facing death, however, man becomes cognizant of the salient characteristic of his existence—its finiteness—and begins to understand his existence. Only then does he live authentically. Hence in the fiction of Sartre and especially of Camus, death is the light bearer—but it always brings "light without radiance."

Since human existence is conditioned by death, it follows that human existence is also characterized by anguish, which is inextricably involved with death. Anguish, the Existentialists are quick to point out, is not synonymous with fear. A person tortured by fear is cognizant of what he fears because it is something definite—cancer, an assailant, going into battle—

---

8 *Myth of Sisyphus*, p. 14.

something that threatens him in some discernible way. Anguish, however, is the fear of Nothingness—a Nothingness that nevertheless is positive and concrete. According to Heidegger, it is that peculiar anxiety of human existence which behooves man to live authentically—that is, in the awareness of Nothingness—and which he suffers when aware of his finiteness. It is not to be equated with the Nothingness of the For-itself in Sartre's orientation, a purely negative concept.

Sartre rather stresses the anguish of freedom and responsibility. Since human existence by definition *is* freedom, man can hardly avoid suffering anguish. For to be free means to project oneself into the future through action, and since there are no reliable moral precedents, no established moral authorities, man is confused and therefore exists in a state of anguish. But this is not all, writes Sartre. First, man's anguish is compounded by responsibility in that he must *create* values for himself through affirmative actions: ". . . if God does not exist, we find no values or commands to turn to which legitimize our conduct. So, in the bright realm of values, we have no excuses behind us, nor justification before us. We are alone, with no excuses. . . . man is condemned to be free. Condemned because he did not create himself, yet, in other respects, is free; because, once thrown into the world, he is responsible for everything he does."[9] Second, man is responsible for actions other than his own. The exemplariness of his every action, in fact, makes him responsible for the actions of all mankind: ". . . our responsibility is much greater than we might have supposed. . . . If I am a workingman and choose to join a Christian trade-union rather than be a communist, and if by being a member I want to show that the best thing for man is resignation, that the kingdom of man is not of this world, I am not only involving my own case—I want to be resigned for everyone. As a result, my action has involved all humanity."[1] This total and deep responsibility is too burdensome to assume and provokes anguish because man dare not move.

These themes, of course, are isolated, skeletal themes, and merely adumbrate the body of Existentialist thought. They represent only the negative aspect of Existentialism, which does not always conclude pessimistically. Neither, as we shall see, does Faulkner. Camus for one took a passionate stand against nihilism, creating from its dregs a way to humanism. Heidegger, despite Sartre's attempt to relegate the German thinker to his own atheistic camp, is more precisely an agnostic, and at the same time his think-

---

[9] *Existentialism*, p. 27.
[1] *Existentialism*, p. 21.

ing is pregnant with religious overtones. But these isolated themes picture the Existentialist world as man awakes to it. Faulkner's world has the same cheerless features. The difference between the two is that whereas the first is defined explicitly, the latter is revealed implicitly.

Like the Existentialist worlds of Sartre, Camus, and Heidegger, Faulkner's world is maintained by no Logos and graced by no Divine Authority. God, to be sure, is suggested occasionally, even referred to in *Go Down, Moses* and *The Unvanquished*. But at best His Person remains a shadow. Substituting for Him is a group of pawn-manipulating and puppeteer gods, the hostile, ambiguous, whimsical gods of doom: the Player (*Light in August* and *Sartoris*), the Umpire (*Intruder in the Dust*), the Judge (*Absalom, Absalom!*), the Cosmic Joker (*The Wild Palms*), and the dark dice-man or stage manager (*The Sound and the Fury*). The personal God of Abraham, Jacob, and Isaac, despite Faulkner's liking for Old Testament parable, is a nebulous memory: that God passed by a long time ago and has since quit the land, "only," as Bon is reported to have said in *Absalom, Absalom!*, "He just didn't think to notify us" (349).

Life in Faulkner's world, as in the Existentialist world, is therefore absurd and nihilistic, a world inhabited by babbling idiots, echoing with sound and fury but signifying nothing. "Without God," even victory is "mockery and delusion" says Brother Fortinbride in *The Unvanquished* (155), echoing Dostoievsky. There are no timeless, universal values here; what "iron old traditions" have existed either "vanish like straws in a gale" (*Absalom, Absalom!*, 207) or render man ineffectual. With the exception of *Big Woods*, in which the wilderness and the past are exalted as meaningful values, Faulkner's characters are confused, rootless, and without identity because there is little they can attach themselves to and depend on. "This whole land," cries Ike McCaslin in "The Bear," "the whole South, is cursed, and all of us who derive from it, whom it ever suckled, white and black both, lie under the curse" (*Go Down, Moses*, 278).

The curse brings spiritual homelessness, an estrangement from moral and cosmic integrity and hence estrangement from oneself. Often this homelessness is treated symbolically. Joe Christmas in *Light in August*, for example, is the illegitimate child of parents he never identifies. Thrown into the world (he is abandoned on the steps of an orphanage), he spends his early years in two different orphanages, his teens on the pharisaical McEachern's farm. Later he is free from all ties, searching for his soul down "the street which was to run for fifteen years. . . . The street ran into

Oklahoma and Missouri and as far south as Mexico and then back north to Chicago and Detroit and then back south again and at last to Mississippi" (195). But in no place "could he be quiet" (197). Like Charles Bon in *Absalom, Absalom!*—"that mental and spiritual orphan whose fate it apparently was to exist in some limbo halfway between where his corporeality was and his mentality and moral equipment desired to be" (124)—Christmas is not wholly black, not wholly white, or at 'least this is what he thinks; like Wilbourne in *The Wild Palms*, who travels from New Orleans "to Chicago and Wisconsin and Chicago and Utah and San Antonio" (311) and finally returns to New Orleans, Christmas's journey terminates at its starting point, the circularity emphasizing his futile search for meaning.

Emancipated by Union soldiers, the Negroes in *The Unvanquished* aimlessly stagger across the countryside, "following and seeking a delusion, a dream, a bright shape which they could not know since there was nothing in their heritage, nothing in the memory even of the old men to tell the others" (92). Young Bayard in *Sartoris* is homeless even among his own family. The Armistice, which brings peace to the world after World War I, ironically precipitates him into despair; he races from Mississippi to Tampico, from Mexico City to Rio, and from San Francisco to Dayton, where he finally meets the destruction toward which he is self-propelled throughout the novel. In *Pylon* Shuman, Laverne, Jiggs, and the parachute jumper are mavericks like Joe Christmas, homeless in Time, drifters who shuttle across the country spending single nights in strange hotels. The Reporter tells Hagood that they have "No ties; no place where you were born and have to go back to it now and then even if it's just only to hate the damn place good and comfortable for a day or two. From coast to coast and Canada in summer and Mexico in winter, with one suitcase and the same canopener . . ." (46). But the anguish of spiritual homelessness, as one might expect, is more excruciatingly felt by the more sensitive characters in Faulkner—Quentin Compson, for example, and the lost Darl: "How often have I lain beneath rain on a strange roof, thinking of home" (*As I Lay Dying*, 396).

Human existence in Faulkner's world is also absurd because man is unwanted, repudiated by the very land he sweats on. Against him, in union with the puppeteer-gods of Fate, is the natural universe. As we have seen, according to Existentialist metaphysics the universe is a dimension of full Being, that density which resists man and provokes nausea in that it makes manifest to the For-itself For-itself's contingency. Indifferent toward man, it is hostile toward man. Similarly, the terrain in Yoknapatawpha County is described in *Intruder in the Dust* as having a "massy intolerable inertia" (174), and in *The Unvanquished* as "possessing . . . that ponderable though passive recalcitrance . . . against which the most brilliant of victories and the most tragic of defeats are but the loud noises of a moment" (3). Crouched in the bowels of Faulkner's County lies an unreasonable, unpredictable primal violence that leaps out of the earth to frustrate and oppose the County's inhabitants again and again—the raging rivers in *As I Lay Dying* and "Old Man," for instance; the dust and oppressive heat which in "Dry September" transform the land into "a bowl of molten lead" (*Collected Stories*, 177) and help perpetrate a lynching. In *Sartoris* young Bayard refers to the earth as Delilah the trickstress, an epithet the tall convict of "Old Man," were he more learned, might well have applied to the waters of the Mississippi River, "that innocent-appearing medium which at one time had held him in iron-like and shifting convolutions like an anaconda" (*Wild Palms*, 145). The land itself, we are told, was created by a "subterranean outrage" (144).

Immersed in absurdity, the Faulknerian unfortunate can hardly delude himself, and he sees no point in deluding his children. There are no fairy tales in Yoknapatawpha County—the young are informed of their futile existence as soon as they are old enough to comprehend it. Addie Bundren in *As I Lay Dying* learned from her father when she was a child that living is difficult, "that the reason for living is getting ready to stay dead" (467), a statement which echoes the proverb cited by Heidegger: "As soon as we are born we are old enough to die." Her childhood education parallels Quentin's in *The Sound and the Fury:* "Father said that a man is the sum of his misfortunes. One day you'd think misfortune would get tired, but then time is your misfortune Father said. . . . You carry the symbol of your frustration into eternity. Then the wings are bigger Father said only who can play a harp" (123). In forcible imagery suggesting that man is a fragile plaything and that even Christ can not save him, Quentin was taught "that all men are just accumulations dolls stuffed with sawdust swept up from the trash heaps where all previous dolls had been thrown away the sawdust flowing from what wound in what side that not for me died not" (194). Bayard Sartoris in *The Unvanquished*, telling the story of his childhood, says that he realized early in life the advisability of joining forces with his boon companion Ringo "against a common enemy, time," to shield themselves against "reality, . . . fact and doom" (4).

In most cases a catechism of doom is superfluous; at instruction time the

young have already been initiated to frustration and death through the
senses. In *As I Lay Dying* Vardaman, the youngest Bundren, sees his mother
die, he smells her rotting body. Before sixteen-year-old Charles Mallison
learns from Gavin Stevens in *Intruder in the Dust* that "tomorrow night is
nothing but one long sleepless wrestle with yesterday's omissions and regrets" (195), he sees the "crushed skull" of Jake Montgomery and recoils
before the "sand clogged into the eyes and nostrils and mouth" of Vinson
Gowrie, who is extricated from quicksand. In the often cited passage from
Absalom, Absalom! young Judith concedes that life is a gift, but one with
strings attached.

> You get born and you try this and you don't know why only you keep
> on trying it and you are born at the same time with a lot of other
> people, all mixed up with them, like trying to, having to, move your
> arms and legs with strings only the same strings are hitched to all the
> other arms and legs and the others all trying and they don't know
> why either except that the strings are all in one another's way like
> five or six people all trying to make a rug on the same loom only
> each one wants to weave his own pattern into the rug. . . . (127)

And in *Pylon*, Jack, Laverne's baby, watches the pilot who may be his father
soar down from the sky like a meteor while his mother screams in his ear.

Hence death in Faulkner is never an abstract concept. It is always ap-
prehended existentially, viewed in connection with one's personal death.
Nor is it a phenomenon that everyone comes to "someday." To exist in
Faulkner's world is to live in the *presence* of death; his world is the existential world in which life and death are inextricable. As Rosa Coldfield
puts it, ". . . *living is one constant and perpetual instant when the arras-
veil before what-is-to-be hangs docile end even glad to the lightest naked
thrust if we dared, were brave enough . . . to make the rending gash*" (*Absalom, Absalom!*, 142-143)—a bit of wisdom she had absorbed at nineteen.
Faulkner's characters can never forget that their lives are bounded by death
because Faulkner does not allow them to forget it: death in his stories is
ubiquitous. Faulkner's own explanation of Quentin's obsession with his
shadow in *The Sound and the Fury* is very much to the point: "I would say
that that shadow that stayed on his mind so much was foreknowledge of
his own death, that he was—Death is here, shall I step into it, or shall I
step away from it a little longer? I won't escape it, but shall I accept it
now or shall I put off until next Friday?"[2]

Take *As I Lay Dying*. In this story Faulkner goes to great lengths to

---

[2] *Faulkner in the University*, p. 2.

accentuate the presence of death. It hovers above the story (the vultures) and behind it (the ominous sound of Cash's hammer banging nails into Addie's coffin). The coffin itself, of course, symbolizes death. Lugged to Jefferson by the Bundrens, Addie's body is a burden; the Bundrens have their cross to bear. *Pylon* is another example. Here death literally and figuratively pervades that atmosphere. The airport, the setting of the story, is a virtual hell: aerobatic planes buzz and crash, hysterical crowds scream and groan like Harpies, the loudspeaker blasts out death notices. A living memorial of death, the Reporter, characterized as having a "ghostlike quality of being beyond all mere restrictions of flesh and time" (171), makes his presence felt almost throughout the novel. His name shrouded in mystery, he is referred to as the "phantom," the "skeleton," the "apparition," and Jiggs jokes that "he looks like they locked the graveyard up before he got in last night" (23). In brief, it's as if all of Faulkner's characters at one time or another have halted before the tombstone of John Sartoris and meditated on its epitaph: "Pause here, son of sorrow; remember death" (*Sartoris,* 375).

Death, the absurd terminus to an absurd existence, is not taken lightly in Faulkner. It is not surprising that his characters exist in anguish: it requires heroic resolve, the Existentialists say, to live in the awareness of one's redoubtable and inescapable Nothingness. It is significant that the more intelligent, sensitive characters in Faulkner's world suffer the most anguish. For as Mr. Compson writes to Quentin at Harvard, ". . . *if aught can be more painful to any intelligence above that of a child or an idiot than a slow and gradual confronting with that which over a long period of bewilderment and dread it has been taught to regard as an irrevocable and unplumbable finality, I do not know it*" (*Absalom, Absalom!*, 173-174). And neither, as it happens, does Quentin. In *The Sound and the Fury*, Quentin realizes that, like "remorse and bereavement," anguish "is not particularly important to the dark diceman" (196), and he commits suicide. Darl, the only member of the Bundren family with any real insight into life (he is mad, but Lear-mad), likewise exists in anguish. He has frequent ontological doubts: "In a strange room you must empty yourself for sleep. And before you are emptied for sleep, what are you. And when you are emptied for sleep, you are not. And when you are filled with sleep, you never were. I don't know what I am. I don't know if I am or not" (*As I Lay Dying*, 396). Musing over Being and Nothingness, however, only intensifies his anguish; his mother's death reminds him of his own finiteness, and in the end he is carted off to an asylum in Jackson. The impassioned Rosa Coldfield, although able, as Quentin and Darl are not, to bear her anguish, asks herself, "Why did I wake since waking I shall never sleep?" (*Absalom, Absalom!*, 143)

But if heroic resolve is required for bearing up under the strain of authentic existence, there are few heroes in Faulkner. Many of his characters decline to live authentically and attempt to quell their anguish by seeking the inviolability of unconsciousness. Without consciousness anguish ceases, man need not tremble in his own Nothingness, he need not accept the responsibility of freedom. But just how does one black out consciousness and yet exist? Suicide takes its own peculiar courage. According to Sartre, man annihilates his consciousness by reducing himself to a material thing—or at least by attempting to. As we have seen, this in fact is the fundamental metaphysical relation between the For-itself and the In-itself, between consciousness and full Being. Consciousness, because insufficient Being, and because aware of its insufficiency, seeks to identify with full Being, to become one with it. This is not to say that the Existentialists condone such action. Indeed, it is regarded as cowardly escapism, as unauthentic living characteristic of "*das Man*" (Heidegger), as living in "bad faith" (Sartre). But nevertheless anguish is intolerable, and man yearns to suppress it. One of Camus' characters realistically expresses man's dilemma as a choice between suicide and "the stupid felicity of stones."

Faulkner's characters attempt to become "things" in devious ways. Not unique with Faulkner's fiction is the unregenerate character who attempts to drink his consciousness under. The elder Jason Compson and the younger Bayard Sartoris, who are conscious of their actions, and Jiggs, who is unconscious of his, are nevertheless alike in that they spend most of their time in senseless stupefaction, fighting anguish with alcohol. The conscience-stricken Gowan in *Requiem for a Nun* would like to destroy himself and, as Gavin Stevens puts it, "plunge into nothing and sink and drown forever and forever, never again to have to remember" (74), but being nerveless he drinks instead. The colloquial phrase "stone drunk" is especially apt here, for these characters actually seek to become unfeeling and unthinking objects.

But because alcohol is not always an effective way of blacking out consciousness, a few of Faulkner's characters seek perpetual sleep. Temple Drake retells the following story of Rider, the protagonist of Faulkner's short story "Pantaloon in Black":

> There was . . . a man . . . before my time in Jefferson . . . His wife had just died—they had been married only two weeks—and he buried her and so at first he tried just walking the country roads at night

for exhaustion and sleep, only that failed and then he tried getting
drunk so he could sleep, and that failed and then he tried fighting
and then he cut a white man's throat with a razor in a dice game and
so at last he could sleep for a little while; which was where the sheriff
found him, asleep on the wooden floor of the gallery of the house
he had rented . . . Only that waked him up, and so in the jail that
afternoon, all of a sudden it took the jailer and a deputy and five
other Negro prisoners just to throw him down and hold him while
they locked the chains on him—lying there on the floor with more
than a half dozen men panting to hold him down, and what do you
think he said? 'Look like I just cant quit thinking. Look like I just
cant quit.' (*Requiem for a Nun*, 198-199)

Other characters fight against consciousness by living on a biological level
only. If they can not reduce themselves to total unconsciousness, at least
they can reduce themselves to animals, which, although conscious, are not
self-conscious. Jiggs in fact is often compared to a dog. He lies on the floor,
curled up, with that "patient inarticulate quality of a dog" (*Pylon*, 188); he
sounds "like a dog" when he chews his food (193).

A more common Faulknerian character, however, flees from anguish
by erecting about him, or allowing to have forced upon him, a life which
is mechanical and specious. He lives according to a "design," a rigid pattern
of action or inaction adopted and maintained in order to forget what is
extraneous to it—namely, authentic existence. Although under a design a man
does not totally surrender his consciousness, he need not be self-conscious
or reflect on reality. Again, the design need not be deliberately adopted,
nor permanent. Bayard Sartoris for example temporally becomes "submerged
in a monotony of days, . . . snarled by a rhythm of activities repeated and
repeated until his muscles grew so familiar with them as to get his body
through the days without assistance from him at all" (*Sartoris*, 204). After
sowing-time he emerges "out of sleep, out of the warm, sunny valleys where
people lived into a region where cold peaks of savage despair stood bleakly
above the lost valleys, among black and savage stars" (205).

An exemplification of the design is the self-imposed quietism of Hightower in *Light in August*. It is also an excellent example of what Sartre says
is the outcome of freedom and responsibility. Man lives in anguish because
his freedom entails the responsibility of legislating values for all humanity;
rather than project into the future, therefore, he abjures his freedom and
remains immobile. This is precisely what Hightower has done. He refuses to
participate in life because, as Byron Bunch points out to him, ". . . a fellow
is more afraid of the trouble he might have than he ever is of the trouble

he's already got" (65). He tries to relieve himself of anguish through reverie, by burying his consciousness in the consciousness of the past. But as long as there is conciousness there is authentic existence—the past has its own anguish. The more complete his quietism, therefore, the better. He attempts to become a thing by secluding himself in his house, wherein he sits, solitary (Byron Bunch is his only visitor and contact with the outside world), a "low oblong shape without any significance at all" (51). He spends his days reposing on a "mute chair evocative of disuse and shabby remoteness from the world, . . . the symbol and the being too of the man himself" (317). He reminds us of Sartre's early disciples who, as the rumor has it, sat rigid and quiet in Paris' *Cafe Flore* after the war, trying to "naught" themselves into objects: "But any day you pass along there [Hightower's house] about dusk or nightfall, you can see him sitting in the window. Just sitting there" (51).

The tall convict of "Old Man" is another character who flees from the responsibility of freedom by means of a design. Dependable, brave, praiseworthy in many ways, his motivation is nevertheless dubious. His first major engagement with the living world—his comical but unfortunate bank robbery attempt—defrauded him of personal values and he consequently has forsaken it. His design consists of the monotonous, routine life of penal occupation governed by clock-time. It is a design because he embraces it. When offered a promotion for good behavior—that is, mechanical behavior—he flatly refuses because the promotion involves a change of routine and the undertaking of responsibilities. When he gains his freedom accidentally, when thrown into the absurd world of imminent death and even greater responsibility, he wishes to "turn his back . . . on all pregnant and female life forever" and makes a superhuman effort to "return to that monastic existence of shotguns and shackles where he would be secure from it" (*Wild Palms*, 153). It is easy for him to abjure his freedom because he never wanted it. He has no desire to give up his consciousness, to be sure; but the monastic existence he leads stimulates "musing impotence" rather than meditation upon himself. Under its mechanical pattern he functions as a robot.

4

The above themes, recurrent in Faulkner's world, are indeed nihilistic, shrouding human existence in gloom. But Faulkner, like some Existentialists, does not conclude in nihilism. The Faulknerian character is neither philosophically determined nor totally defenseless. Thrown into the world without his volition, he nevertheless is free, as Heidegger would say, to discard his "thrownness" (*Geworfenheit*), to permit it to frustrate him, or—as in the case of Ike McCaslin, Byron Bunch, Dilsey and others—seize it, grapple with it, and force it to yield meaning. But he can prevail only if he acknowledges and stands up to the fierce grimace of authentic existence.

From the standpoint of positive philosophy, Faulkner and the Existentialists take an adamant stand against irresponsibility and life-denial. Both Faulkner and Sartre believe in an ethics of total involvement. "The doctrine I am presenting," the latter writes, "is the very opposite of quietism, since it declares. 'There is no reality except in action.' "[3] Just so, Hightower's life is a failure because any one action or situation is not total involvement. When he finally commits himself to life and champions Joe Christmas, it is too late; in the end he is destroyed. But the present, Faulkner holds, is not the individual's only responsibility. Past, present, and future being inseparable, he is responsible for all three, which are actually one. Temple Drake, for example, comes to learn that the murder Nancy Mannigoe perpetrates in *Requiem for a Nun* is connected with "that morning eight years ago when I got on the train at the University" (209), an event which sparks the grotesque action of *Sanctuary*; and Ringo in *The Unvanquished* notes that the "first batch of mules we got for nothing" (211) kills Granny—not Ab Snopes or Grumby, who is the immediate cause of her death. Unless he accepts the past, the individual has no future, for the one is created out of the other. The future, that is to say, is being lived in the present. In this respect Faulkner is closer to Camus than to Sartre: Sartre insists that man's essence, his meaning, lies in the future *which is continuously ahead of him*; Faulkner and Camus contend that the future ahead of man is not a reality except as it is lived in the present, and that man achieves meaning only by living the moment dynamically. There is no tomorrow for Faulkner and Camus because there is always a tomorrow.

There is, however, one important difference between Faulkner's world and the world of the French Existentialists. Richard Lehan has rightly remarked that unlike the Sartre-Camus world, Faulkner's world at one time was morally centered.[4] During the pioneer days in Yoknapatawpha County, before the white man applied his instruments to the Redman's land and measured it off to argue over and bequeath, before he brought slavery into

---

[3] *Existentialism*, p. 37.
[4] "Existentialism and the Modern American Novel," unpublished dissertation (Wisconsin, 1959), pp. 197-198. Richard Lehan and I, working independently, have arrived at similar conclusions. I am grateful for having had the opportunity to read his dissertation.

the territory—in short, before what must be called a secular Fall, Faulkner's
world was unified in some sort of Logos. The world of Sartre and Camus,
however, has never been balanced or blessed; it is given as nihilistic.

For this reason it seems to me that Faulkner's world, in its orientation,
more closely approximates Heidegger's than the Sartre-Camus world. Although Heidegger does not give credence to God, his world is centered in
Being, from which, he believes, philosophy has been estranged historically
and man ontologically. Being for Heidegger is not to be equated with what
Sartre means by Being. It is to be understood in the pre-Socratic sense of
wonder. Neither *a* being (an object) nor the beingness of Being ("horse-
ness is the whatness of horse"), it is the all-inclusive totality of all there is.
For Heidegger Being is also Truth, Truth understood in the Greek sense
of *aletheia*: unhiddenness. Being reveals itself through man, in man's openness to it. I describe Heidegger's idea of Being because it seems to me that
Faulkner's aim is to allow Being, as Heidegger understands it, to reveal
itself, to manifest itself through the consciousness of his characters.

Whether or not Faulkner is cognizant of Heidegger's idea of Being, or
of Existentialism as such, is, I think, irrelevant to his existential affinities.
They no doubt stem in part from his sympathy with the Hebraic moral tradition, which, like Existentialism, stresses an ethics of action, guilt, and man's
finiteness; and with Dostoievsky, whose psychological insight into the nature
of suffering and the human condition anticipated existential dogma. But
Hebraism and Dostoievsky have influenced him only because they reflect
modern man's travail and the modern world as it reveals itself. The modern
world has priority: hence his Existentialist affinities. William Barrett writes
that

> the themes that obsess both modern art and existential philosophy
> are the alienation and strangeness of man in his world; the contra-
> dictoriness, feebleness, and contingency of human existence; the
> central and overwhelming reality of time for man who has lost his
> anchorage in the eternal.
>   The testimony art brings to these themes is all the more convinc-
> ing in that it is spontaneous; it does not spring from ideas or from
> any intellectual program.[5]

Faulkner, it is now clear, is not writing about little people in a little county
in Mississippi. Neither is he writing about the Hellenic world Narcissa in
Sartoris ruefully ponders in a book—a "world where things happened as
they should happen" (259). He is writing about the modern world, and

---

[5] *Irrational Man*, p. 56.

his response to it is similar to the Existentialist's response simply because they live in the same confused world, from which the Holy has vanished. There are indeed churches in Yoknapatawpha County, but as Hightower painfully remarks, someone has "removed the bells from their steeples" (426).

Editions Cited

Sartoris, Harcourt, Brace, 1929

The Sound and the Fury and *As I Lay Dying*, Modern Library, 1946

Light in August, Modern Library, 1950

Pylon, Harrison Smith and Robert Haas, 1935

Absalom, Absalom!, Random House, 1936, or Modern Library, 1951

The Unvanquished, Random House, 1938

The Wild Palms, Random House, 1939

The Hamlet, Random House, 1940

Go Down, Moses, Random House, 1943, or Modern Library, 1955

Intruder in the Dust, Random House, 1948

Collected Stories, Random House, 1950

Requiem for a Nun, Random House, 1951

A Fable, Random House, 1954